Break Your Burnout Cycle

Break Your Burnout Cycle
*A Woman's Five-Step Guide To a
Thriving Career Journey*

Kai-Nneka Townsend

Copyright © 2022 - Kai-Nneka Townsend - All rights reserved.

The content contained within this book may not be reproduced, duplicated or transmitted without direct written permission from the author or the publisher.

Under no circumstances will any blame or legal responsibility be held against the publisher, or author, for any damages, reparation, or monetary loss due to the information contained within this book, either directly or indirectly.

Legal Notice:

This book is copyright protected. It is only for personal use. You cannot amend, distribute, sell, use, quote or paraphrase any part, of the content within this book, without the consent of the author or publisher.

Disclaimer Notice:

Please note the information contained within this document is for educational and entertainment purposes only. All effort has been executed to present accurate, up to date, reliable, complete information. No warranties of any kind are declared or implied. Readers acknowledge that the author is not engaged in the rendering of legal, financial, medical or professional advice. The content within this book has been derived from various sources. Please consult a licensed professional before attempting any techniques outlined in this book.

By reading this document, the reader agrees that under no circumstances is the author responsible for any losses, direct or indirect, that are incurred as a result of the use of the information contained within this document, including, but not limited to, errors, omissions, or inaccuracies.

Contents

Introduction viii
    Lost in Ambition 1

Am I Really in Burnout? 6
    What Is Burnout? 7
    Five Stages of Burnout 10
    What Are Your Triggers? 16
    What to Do About It 22

Step 1: Act Now—Build Your Short-Term Recovery Plan .. 24
    Get Out of Your Comfort Zone 25
    Create Your Short-Term Burnout Recovery Plan 27

Step 2: Reset the Dial in Your Life—Relax! The Building Won't Collapse Without You 34
    The Clean Out 35
    Three Types of Burnout Recovery 37
    Identify Perfectionism 39

The Check-In 43

Beyond Work-Life Balance 50

Your Time Out Action Plan 52

Step 3: Invoke Your Inner Warrior—Reignite Your Passion for Your Career Goals 56

Finding Your Groove at Work 57

Create a New Template 64

Let Your Inner Warrior Speak Up 68

To Quit or Not to Quit? 72

Step 4: Stand Your Ground—No Backsies! 78

Making It Work for You 79

Become a Builder 97

Practice Grace With Your Pace 102

Step 5: End the Burnout Cycle—Evaluate Your New Path . . 110

Questions to Ask Yourself 111

How to Choose a Coach, Therapist, or Other Helping Professional 122

Bonus Chapter: Managing a Team in Burnout 128

Signs of Burnout in Employees 129

Burnout-Busting Strategies to Implement at Work 132

Watch Your Words 134

Conclusion 138

About The Author 145

References 147

Image References. 157

Introduction

*We're totally guilty of doing too much at once,
all while trying to manage the noise in our heads that
says we're not doing enough.*

Vanessa Autrey

Lost in Ambition

Becoming a successful woman was always a part of my plan. From as early as 10 years old, I remember telling anyone who would listen that I was going to travel the world and work for "BIG" companies. My family encouraged me to pursue these big goals and by the age of 17, I was out of the house and globe-trotting for my studies and work.

There I was, this young Black woman, taking charge in every space that I entered. Saying that I felt on top of the world is perhaps an understatement. Life was finally happening *for* me and many of those career opportunities that were penciled inside my journal were coming to fruition.

I worked mostly in male-dominated environments and quickly moved up the ranks in my career. Over the span of 15 years, I had filled positions in several industries like public and social health, international development, railway, and project management. It was an honor to receive recognition for my expertise, but truth be told, the best part was knowing that despite being one of few female leaders, I was holding my own in that space, overcoming a lot of the corporate adversity women face as they rise up the ranks.

Anyone watching my career journey would've thought I had it all, and I'll admit that I often carried myself as though I did. But what many were unaware of was that I was battling chronic fatigue and stress, and I didn't have a harmonious work-life balance. For more than a decade, my life was centered around work. I practically lived in the office, which meant that other areas of my life were being neglected.

For about a year or so, I brushed off the fatigue and stress as symptoms that were "part of the job." I was reluctant to open up about them because the last thing I wanted was for people to think I was ungrateful—or worse, incompetent at the job.

So, like any other woman in the business environment who is deathly afraid of being undermined, I kept my mouth shut and pushed through! My body took the physical strain up to a point. Eventually, waking up each morning became difficult. It felt like I was carrying a heavy rock on my back and no amount of rest could alleviate the pressure.

But that was only the beginning of the snowballing effect. Soon enough, my physical exhaustion triggered emotional issues like being overly sensitive to criticism, feeling overwhelmed with my work commitments, and doubting my capacity to lead (also known as imposter syndrome). I had become my own worst nightmare—and it didn't help that the inner critic reminded me of my ineffectiveness every chance it got.

After a year of feeling like I was losing myself to my job, a mentor suggested that I may be experiencing burnout. She described it as a state of mental, emotional, and physical exhaustion because of workplace stress. Some of the symptoms that I was displaying, like chronic fatigue, feeling isolated from others, and being very cynical about my job, were common signs of burnout. It was such a relief to find out that I wasn't going crazy and that what I was experiencing was common, particularly for women.

One of the biggest myths about burnout is that it is somehow your fault. If you feel burned out, then the assumption is that you are willingly piling on more work for yourself. But a greater workload could only be one factor causing your burnout. The main reason behind burnout is how you define what is important in your life, and the ability to apply your focus and energies proportionately to them, putting the right boundaries in place around work, health, personal life, etc. What you do between 9-to-5 does not have to become who you are. Your life is multifaceted and there are many different parts that somehow need to come together in perfect harmony for you to feel successful.

A survey completed by over 1,000 employees in the United States and the United Kingdom showed that 68% of women experienced burnout within the past seven days, compared to 50% of men who reported the same (Elsesser, 2022). One of the reasons cited for this "exhaustion gap" was the increased pressure on women to take care of their parenting responsibilities on the one hand and fight to stay ahead of the game in their careers on the other.

This pressure can be traced back to the time when women were starting to enter the corporate space. Many of the early working women felt like they were trading motherhood by going into a male-dominated environment. For them, it was either a life spent as a housewife, or a life spent climbing the corporate ladder. Still today, there are many women whose devotion to work causes an imbalance in other areas of their lives. This is usually the trigger that sets off burnout.

The more I studied the cause and effects of burnout, the more courage I gained to challenge my inner critic and rediscover what meaningful work meant for me. My burnout wasn't a result of incompetence or overambition; it was actually a cry for help. I had been suppressing my mental, emotional, and physical needs for many years, at the expense of climbing the corporate ladder.

This book is dedicated to women, like me, who are go-getters and aren't afraid of the grind, but may feel like they are at a crossroads in their life. On the one hand, they want to continue pursuing everything they want in life—a successful career, a thriving personal life, and a budding business—but on the other hand have thoughts about giving it all up because it all just feels like too much.

To stay ahead of the game and achieve your goals, you must avoid or break free from the burnout cycle—and root out other behaviors associated with it, like imposter syndrome, self-sabotage, and goalless productivity.

After reading this book, you will be able to clearly recognize burnout, be equipped with effective coping strategies to recover from it and stop it from happening again. Furthermore, you will regain your big "WHY" and have the confidence to determine the next best steps for your career journey.

Burnout might feel like the end of the road, but rest assured, it is in fact the beginning of a new one!

Am I Really in Burnout?

I'm tired, inevitably. But it's more than that. I'm hollowed out. I'm tetchy and irritable, constantly feeling like prey, believing that everything is urgent and that I can never do enough.

Katherine May

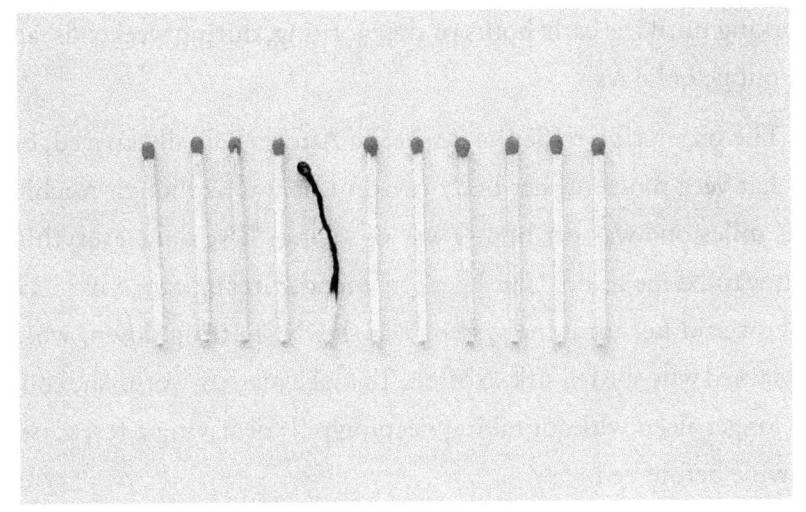

What Is Burnout?

Tanya resigned from her law firm weeks after being promoted as Senior Associate Attorney and receiving the highest achiever award. She started out as a paralegal, helping the firm's finest lawyers prepare documents for trials, and secretly she hated her job due to the number of hours it demanded. What Tanya wanted more than anything was to start her own law firm and have enough time on her hands to focus on her family. But in order to achieve this goal, she was prepared to work harder than everyone else. For the next six years, she worked tirelessly to prove to others that she could be successful.

The burnout started around year five when Tanya pretty much lived in the office. There wasn't a learning opportunity that slipped past her, and a great deal of her time was spent nurturing work relationships. Now, if this was a healthy work environment, it wouldn't keep her working until the early hours of the morning, during weekends, and on public holidays.

The promotion to Senior Associate Attorney finally arrived, but at that very moment, her body caved in. It was as though reaching this milestone was her body's way of saying, "I've done everything you wanted me to do. Can I get some tender loving care now?" The doctor said her immune system was slowly shutting down, which explained why she fell sick so often. To make matters worse, she could no longer sleep without taking sleeping pills or having a few glasses of wine before bed.

She came to the sobering realization that her life was centered around work, and if she didn't find balance now, who knows how much worse her overall well-being would get? Following advice from a coach, she took two weeks off work to focus on other areas of her life. But after those two weeks, it became clear that the over-investment in her job was the actual cause of her ailments. What she needed was to reevaluate what mattered most in her life and make time for all of those things.

According to the World Health Organization (WHO), burnout can be defined as "a syndrome conceptualized as resulting from chronic workplace stress that has not been successfully managed" (World Health Organization, 2019). It is characterized by three dimensions, which are:

- A state of physical, mental, and emotional exhaustion.
- Reduced sense of accomplishment and productivity at work.
- Increased mental detachment and cynicism related to one's job.

Technically, burnout is not seen as a medical condition; however, it can lead to physiological and mental health conditions, such as chronic fatigue, heart disease, insomnia, anxiety, and depression. Not only that, but burnout can also cause psychological issues that affect one's sense of self. Working women, in particular, are more prone to burnout due to their struggles of balancing work life with home life, and everything else in between! Added to this, climbing up the corporate ladder does not come without its own stressors, as many women fight for equity and recognition for their contributions at work.

The fact that the medical community doesn't recognize burnout as a serious medical condition contributes to the stigma that often exists around it. Research has shown that those suffering from burnout are more likely to be seen as incompetent than those who do not report experiencing burnout (May et al., 2020).

In 2020, during the peak of the pandemic, a video of a doctor falling in and out of sleep while walking to his car made the rounds on social media. Closed-circuit television (CCTV) footage followed the doctor until he reached the underground parking. At that point, he collapsed on the ground as a result of extreme exhaustion. This video sparked a conversation about the silent killer amongst doctors—burnout. Even though studies tell us that over half of medical doctors experience burnout and the most vulnerable are those in the emergency room (ER) and intensive care units, doctors still feel a lot of shame in admitting and seeking support for burnout (May et al., 2020).

The shame in admitting burnout doesn't start at the hospitals. It begins during medical school when doctors feel pressured to excel and prove themselves. Medical students go through rigorous training and studying to qualify as doctors. The nature of this training is so intense that many students who enroll in medical school either drop out or take longer to complete their degrees. As a result, successful medical students develop a sense of inadequacy.

Sure, they graduated and passed many of their modules, but this doesn't eradicate the pressure to level up and perform above average when they start working. Take this, coupled with not receiving enough positive reinforcement on the job, and you have a trainee doctor who is overburdened with caring for patients, but wouldn't dare to show any signs of overt frustration.

Five Stages of Burnout

When many people explain burnout, they describe it as feeling stressed or tired at work. Even though work-related stress and exhaustion can be symptoms of burnout, it can go beyond this. In the literal sense, burnout is emptying all the fuel you have in your tank. Not only are you maxed out at work, but also in your personal relationships, physical health, social life, and other areas of your life.

Imagine driving a car with a full tank of gas on a long-distance journey. During the first few hours, you are cruising on the highway, singing along to your favorite jams and taking in the beauty of the open road. Eventually, the tank will run low, but that doesn't mean you need to stop—it is just a reminder to stop at your nearest gas station and get a refill. After the fifth hour, the orange light might turn on. Making a quick stop at a gas station is now critical, rather than optional.

If you ignore this warning, the orange light will turn red, and your car will lose most of its power. The brake pads will feel a lot heavier to push down and you won't be able to cruise at the same speed you were accustomed to. You may even start to feel frustrated about driving such a long distance.

That open road that seemed poetic a few hours ago looks dull and never-ending. The music playing on the stereo gets on your nerves, but so does the silence that occupies the car when you switch it off. Nothing will feel enjoyable until gas is pumped into the car, and you can start driving normally again.

The car analogy is a great illustration of what happens when you cruise through life without achieving balance in the different areas. One or two areas often take precedence in your life causing you to burn all your energy on them. There is no way to refill this energy, so now you are unable to pursue other areas of your life.

Your tank doesn't get empty immediately. It can take several months or years. But one way of identifying burnout is by understanding the five stages of burnout: the honeymoon phase, onset of stress, chronic stress, burnout, and habitual burnout (The Calmer Team, 2020). Below is a look at each stage and the common symptoms that may arise.

Stage 1: Honeymoon Phase

When you start a new job or strive to achieve a career-related goal, it is common to experience an increase in job satisfaction. You don't need an extra push to get up early in the morning, think on your feet, and display full commitment at work. You can experience somewhat of a "high" engaging with coworkers or demonstrating leadership, which makes what you do feel meaningful.

Although stress may be prevalent in this initial stage of burnout, it is usually associated with your standards of performance, like going above and beyond to ensure that a presentation looks outstanding. Below are some of the symptoms you may experience during the honeymoon phase:

- increased commitment to work tasks
- motivation to do your best
- spontaneous ideas and creativity
- increased productivity
- sustained energy levels

It is often said that employing healthy coping strategies is all it takes to sustain the honeymoon phase and prevent burnout. However, this is easier said than done. In most cases, the "high" of the honeymoon phase is so intoxicating that we are willing to give more of ourselves to feel even better about our work.

Stage 2: Onset of Stress

After several months or years of adrenaline, your motivation to function at your optimum level can become weaker and weaker. This isn't due to laziness, but more so coming to terms with the reality of being a top performer in your company or industry. To put it in simple words, being the best comes at a price. Once you discover what that price is, you may start to feel the weight of your ambitions on your shoulders. Here are a few symptoms you may experience at this stage:

- increased anxiety
- reluctance to make decisions
- high blood pressure/heart palpitations (or other physiological symptoms)
- forgetfulness
- neglecting your personal needs
- changes in appetite
- reduced quality of sleep

What's important to note about the onset of stress is the changes to your lifestyle. This is perhaps one of the major warning signs that you may have an unhealthy relationship with your work. Ideally, work-related tasks should only be carried out during clearly defined office hours, and the rest of the day should be spent taking care of other personal responsibilities. Setting work boundaries can reverse the onset of stress and ensure that your professional life doesn't impede on your personal life.

Stage 3: Chronic Stress

From the third stage onward, there is a lot of pressure placed on your physical, mental, and emotional well-being. Moreover, the dedication you have shown to the one area of your life, like your love for your job, turns into resentment because you are not feeling adequately rewarded for the commitment you demonstrate. A few common symptoms of chronic stress include:

- overt or covert angry behavior
- acts of sabotage like missing work deadlines
- chronic fatigue
- pessimistic attitude
- lack of interest in hobbies or interests outside of work
- social withdrawal from friends and family
- increased caffeine, drug, alcohol, or prescription medication intake

Another clear warning sign of chronic stress is feeling anxious when preparing for work in the mornings. You may experience heart palpitations, feel demotivated, or get headaches just thinking about commuting to work. Like the orange light that flashes when a car is running on low fuel, these physical symptoms are your body's way of communicating physical and emotional distress. The temptation that many fall prey to is to mask these symptoms by self-medicating, but that won't make them go away. The best thing to do when experiencing chronic stress is to take some time off and allow the mind and body to recharge.

Stage 4: Burnout

The symptoms of stress you experience reach critical levels when you get to stage four. In many cases, taking time off work is not enough to address the psychological issues that manifest, such as feeling empty inside or depressed. Remember, burnout is more than tiredness. It is feeling physically, mentally, and emotionally depleted. Even someone who would normally have a high tolerance for stress is likely to show signs of distress when they become burned out. Common symptoms that may occur include:

- chronic migraines
- mental dissociation
- emotional withdrawal from others
- obsession with work-related problems
- weakened immune system
- regular digestive problems
- desire to escape or isolate from others

Typical coping strategies to deal with stress may not be effective when managing burnout. You will need a holistic approach that caters to both physical and psychological needs. If you suspect that you are suffering from related mental health conditions, then you may also need to explore additional treatment options like psychotherapy or prescription medication.

Stage 5: Habitual Burnout

Ideally, burnout shouldn't be left until it reaches the fifth and final stage. Burnout may not even be the worst health condition you are suffering; you may be exposed to other severe chronic issues that compromise your daily functioning like substance abuse, depression, suicidal thoughts, or other behavioral issues. The worst-case scenario is that your physical and psychological issues interfere with your life to the extent that you get hospitalized. Seeking medical assistance is not optional at this stage, since doctors are the only ones qualified to offer you the best treatment plan.

What Are Your Triggers?

When completing my graduate degree, I remember sitting in lecture halls with mostly male students. Since I was so passionate about my degree, I didn't pay too much attention to it. After all, being male or female wasn't a good indicator of competence—or was it?

When I started working, it became apparent that I would be one of the few women in the office and on various teams, and that the more prestigious the job title was, the fewer women were represented. I found myself spending evenings on Google, searching: *How to have more influence in the workplace as a woman*. I get it. It was quite desperate of me. However, I felt an increasing pressure to be exceptional at my job so that being a woman wouldn't count against me.

Both men and women experience burnout at work, but the reasons that trigger burnout in women are unique. For me, the lack of racial and gender representation at work meant that I would need to be an outlier in order to gain the same recognition as my peers. In the rail industry where I worked for several years, I felt responsible for debunking stereotypes about women holding positions of leadership and leading male-dominated teams. Since men are more likely to be considered for positions of leadership, they don't have to constantly worry about whether they are doing enough to prove their competence.

Even in workplace environments where there aren't visible biases, women generally hold themselves to a greater standard than men. We are afraid of making mistakes that only feed into the stereotype that a woman's place is in the kitchen, not inside a boardroom. The workplace is filled with different women, occupying a variety of positions. Each woman has her own story of why she feels the need to over-achieve and prove their worth. Below are some of the common triggers of burnout that many working women cite:

1. Parenthood

Being a parent is a full-time job and requires the participation of both mothers and fathers. However, research continues to show a gender gap in parenting. A study investigating the parenting of dual-earner couples found that fathers spend roughly 7 hours per week on childcare compared to mothers who spend roughly 14 hours (Schoppe-Sullivan, 2017). The active participation of mothers was most evident when their children were still young; they were more likely to spend twice as much time on childcare than their spouses.

But in modern times, parenting is not the only work that mothers perform. Many of them are still responsible for doing most of the house chores and reporting to the office five days a week. In fact, the same study showed that once a woman became a parent, their total workload increased by 21 hours per week (Schoppe-Sullivan, 2017).

In comparison, when a man became a parent, his total workload only increased by 12.5 hours per week. This finding showed that parenthood alone brought about a 70% increase in responsibility for women than men, which contributes to the work-related stress many women succumb to.

2. Compassion Fatigue

Empathy is the ability to place yourself in another person's shoes and understand their experience from their perspective. There is a common stereotype that women are wired to show more empathy than men, but research has shown that it is a skill both genders are capable of developing. Gender differences in displaying empathy have to do with willpower, cultural expectations, and traditional gender roles. Studies also show that women are more likely to display empathy as part of their motivation to move ahead in their careers and build strong work relationships (Nicklin, 2020). However, this tendency also makes women vulnerable to compassion fatigue, which occurs when helping others becomes mentally and emotionally exhausting.

3. Underrepresentation

There are more women in the workplace than there were two decades ago. Companies that prioritize diversity and inclusivity tend to focus on hiring a diverse team of people and making sure that marginalized groups are represented at all levels of the company, including leadership roles. However, this is still not the norm. Women are less likely to be considered for promotion into managerial positions than men.

This typically leads to overqualified women feeling stuck in their current positions, with skills they cannot use. The lack of career development opportunities and inclusivity policies at work means that women must work twice as hard as men to be recognized for great work and given the chance to prove their leadership capabilities. Women who are overlooked by their managers can become stressed and frustrated by covert discrimination.

4. Imposter Syndrome

Imposter syndrome is defined as the chronic feeling of not being good enough. Researchers have found that both men and women can suffer from this mental distortion; however, when the term was first introduced, it was used to describe the experience of female workers doubting their capabilities and feeling like they don't belong in the workplace environment.

For many women, the cause of imposter syndrome has to do with traditional gender roles and being conditioned from a young age to not pursue goals that were considered "masculine," such as aspiring to be a leader. Even though women are now accepted into the once male-dominated corporate environment, they still struggle to reconcile the identity they were brought up to accept and their true selves, with all of their many talents and skills. Feeling like an imposter can make many women overwork themselves as a way of proving to their colleagues that they deserve to be there.

5. Income Inequality

Another form of gender-based discrimination at work that leads to increased stress levels is the pay gap between men and women. It has been well documented that men are paid considerably more than women at work. In the United States, research shows that women are paid 82 cents for every dollar earned by a man (Leisenring, 2020). The pay gap widens depending on a woman's age, race, marital status, and educational background.

For example, a White young woman without children holding a university degree will potentially earn more than a non-White single mother who is in mid-life and doesn't hold a degree. But still, neither of the women are likely to earn more than a White man in a lesser job role. Knowing that you are potentially underselling yourself is frustrating, especially when you are carrying most of the financial burden for your family. Other external economic pressures, such as the rise of gas and food prices, add to the stress and anxiety women feel to earn more income.

6. Intersectionality

Women who are marginalized, meaning they are underrepresented in every sphere of society, are vulnerable to burnout. Examples of marginalized groups in the workplace include members of the LGBTQIA+ community, disabled people, and non-White racial groups. These women enter a male or White dominated workplace environment, usually being the only or one of a few women like them. To compete with male or White coworkers, they often need to perform beyond their scope of work.

Many of the sacrifices they make are unrewarded because it is expected of them to earn their respect and influence at work. Women who fit under more than one marginalized group, such as being Black and disabled, or Asian and part of the LGBTQIA+ community, face challenges at each of those intersections and need to work that much harder to get to the next level.

7. Loss of Passion

It is common to experience burnout when you are no longer passionate about your job. This could be due to many factors unrelated to your work, such as developing new interests, taking on new personal responsibilities like being a parent, or not feeling challenged enough in your current capacity. As you will learn in a later chapter, it is possible to reignite the passion for your job, but if you don't see yourself growing in that company or field, then it may be time to change jobs or undergo a career transition.

Reflect on the triggers mentioned above. Which ones apply to you? How have they made your career progression that much harder?

What to Do About It

Experiencing burnout does not foreshadow the end of your career. It is simply your mind and body's way of getting your attention, so you can reflect on your current work-life balance and reevaluate your priorities. At some point in your career, you absolutely loved your work. It gave your life meaning, and this made you feel good about yourself. It is possible to change your life and get back to that place of feeling passionate about your work, without disinvesting in other areas too. However, to do so requires that you follow five steps, which include:

STEP 1: Act now

STEP 2: Reset the dial in your life

STEP 3: Invoke your inner warrior

STEP 4: Stand your ground

STEP 5: End the burnout cycle

Look at the first letter of each step. What word does it spell? That's right. *ARISE*. The acronym is intentional because it highlights something that many of us misunderstand about burnout: We can overcome it. It is understandable why anyone would want to throw in the towel and quit their jobs when suffering from burnout, but taking these measures isn't always necessary.

Of course, there are some instances where quitting your job and focusing on recovery is the best thing to do. Even if that is the path you take, know that you have what it takes to arise from the slump you are in, regain the lost momentum, and continue chasing after your career goals, having new parameters in place!

For the remainder of this book, you will be taken through this five-step process that will enable you to *ARISE* and combat burnout. These steps helped me overcome burnout and start a new chapter of passion and growth in my career without constantly returning to the cycle of burnout!

As you grow through the five steps, remember that your career journey is unique. There may be thousands of other professionals working in your company, but what motivates you to wake up in the morning and dedicate yourself to work is completely different. These five steps provide a framework that you can customize and make your own so that ultimately, you can achieve the success you desire without compromising your well-being.

Without further ado, let us jump straight into the first step!

STEP 1

Act Now—Build Your Short-Term Recovery Plan

> *Start right now with whatever you have.*
> *Six months from now it will be an absolute game-changing move of your life.*
>
> Hiral Nagda

Get Out of Your Comfort Zone

In the previous chapter, we discussed the five stages of burnout and observed the common triggers. Ideally, you want to catch the symptoms of burnout before you reach stage three, so that you can start implementing a short-term recovery plan. In essence, the earlier you intervene, the easier it will be to manage the effects of burnout on your own.

Now, I get it. Starting anything is tough, especially when you are taken out of your comfort zone. Treating burnout requires you to have an open mind and be willing to try out strategies that you may have never considered before. It will make you feel like a student again, relying on an abundance of new skills and knowledge to get your health in check. My advice is to embrace the moments of uncertainty and see the opportunities presented as you step outside of your comfort zone.

The very first thing you will need to prepare for the incredible journey of healing ahead is an attitude audit. This means having an honest conversation with yourself about the purpose of this journey and the kind of mindset you will need to persevere through challenging times. If your attitude is not right, you will find it harder to accept suggestions and look at your current lifestyle from a different perspective. Below are a few questions to assess whether you are mentally in the right place to break the burnout cycle:

Are you willing to take ownership of behaviors that may have led to compromising your overall well-being?

- Are you prepared to invest your time and effort in making lifestyle adjustments, even when it takes longer to see results?
- Do you have a compelling vision for what your desired workplace environment looks and feels like?
- Are you willing to be fearless in standing up for yourself at work and enforcing healthy work boundaries?
- Are you prepared to distance yourself from negative influences (i.e., People, social media, addictive substances,

junk food, etc.) both at work and in your personal life?

- Are you prepared to hold yourself accountable throughout this process and take regular breaks to reflect on your thoughts and behaviors?
- Are you ready to make self-care a priority in your life and be quicker at responding to your physical, mental, and emotional needs?

If your answers to the questions above are a resounding, "YES," then you have passed the attitude audit! It is now time to take action and create your short-term burnout recovery plan.

Create Your Short-Term Burnout Recovery Plan

Imagine there is a small fire starting in your kitchen. How do you put out the flames?

One option is to call the local fire department and request a few firefighters to bring their tools and put the fire out. This option would work, except the fire is growing stronger by the minute. Another option is to call your six-foot-tall, Thor-built neighbor, and ask him to demonstrate a heroic act by putting out the flames.

Once again, this option is great, but by the time you have explained the situation and pleaded for them to help you, the fire would have spread to other parts of the kitchen. The most practical and immediate approach is to look around the room and find supplies that you can use to put out the fire on your own. If this wasn't an emergency, you wouldn't have to be the one addressing the issue.

The moment you discover symptoms of burnout, the clock starts ticking. You don't have a lot of time before one stage of burnout leads to the next, and within months, you are in a worse position. You want to remove yourself as far away as possible from the danger zone, which begins with chronic stress.

The short-term burnout recovery plan helps you do just that. It is your custom plan that includes emergency coping strategies to address the burnout triggers identified in Chapter 1. The purpose of your recovery plan is to target specific areas of your life where you are feeling overburdened with responsibility and bring immediate relief. Once your situation has stabilized, you can then proceed to carry out the long-term recovery strategies that will be discussed in the following chapters.

Grab a big sheet of paper, some colorful markers, and any other craft supplies you have at home. Look through the coping strategies listed below and create your targeted short-term recovery plan.

1. Eat Well

Food can have the same effect as medicine on an ailing body. However, the trick is knowing what kinds of foods to consume. In general, you want to stay away from comfort foods, like fried meats, pasta dishes, and cheesy pizzas, as they can leave you feeling sluggish.

You may also want to avoid mood-altering foods with caffeine and sugar, which give you an instant buzz followed by a crash. Structure your diet around whole foods (preferably sourced from the earth and with minimal processing). These may include a variety of fruits, leafy green vegetables, whole grains, nuts and seeds, and smaller portions of fresh free-range protein.

2. Exercise

Increasing physical activity during burnout may seem counterintuitive. However, studies have shown that moderate cardio workouts, like walking, swimming, or doing aerobic exercises, can alleviate mental exhaustion, increase central nervous system response, and improve cognitive performance (Millard, 2021). Moreover, working out makes you feel good about yourself. Research shows that a 20-30-minute aerobic workout can trigger the release of brain chemicals known as endorphins, which carry the same potent feeling as morphine (Daly, 2020).

3. Sleep Well

One of the major lifestyle causes of burnout is not getting adequate sleep. Sleep deprivation, which is defined as sleeping for less than six hours a night, can be attributed to on-the-job tiredness, irritability, and anxiety. One of the natural ways to improve sleep is to put yourself on a sleeping routine. This means going to bed and getting up in the morning at the same time, so your brain can learn the new sleep-wake rhythm. However, your routine can also include relaxation rituals that you perform before bed, such as meditating, drinking chamomile tea, and switching off all electronics. These rituals are supposed to help you feel sleepy leading up to your bedtime.

4. Schedule Downtime for Yourself

As someone who lives a busy life, it is important to have a moment during the day when you can retreat and spend time by yourself. Find a secluded room or area in your house, free from technological devices and any other distractions. You can use this time to take a power nap, read a chapter from a book, listen to a motivational podcast, or check in with yourself. The focus of your quiet times should remain on you, not your work or family commitments. If you enjoy journaling, you can take the opportunity to write down any pressing thoughts or emotions in your mind.

5. Make Small Changes

It may not be practical to switch up your lifestyle completely. For example, you may want to incorporate more physical exercise into your routine, but due to your work schedule aren't able to. Find small 5–10-minute gaps in your daily calendar to practice some of these healthy habits. I know the thought of exercising for five minutes doesn't seem like much, but when you find a few of these gaps during the day, they add up! Furthermore, since making small changes doesn't require a lot of investment of your time, you will find that there is a low amount of resistance when it is time to perform them.

6. Recraft Your Job

In the short-term, it won't be easy to reduce your workload. Nonetheless, you can adjust the importance of your daily tasks, so you can prioritize tasks that add the most value. A technique that can help you redefine your work tasks is the 80/20 rule. This rule states that 20% of your daily tasks add 80% of value. In other words, if you have 10 tasks to complete in a day, two of them would be classified as extremely important. Look at your work schedule and identify the 20% that brings in 80% of value. Start each workday by prioritizing these tasks, so that even if you don't complete the remaining tasks, at least you have made a lot of progress!

7. Meditate

You don't need to be spiritual to practice meditation. In the Western world, meditation is considered a mind therapy that can clear your head and induce a sense of calm. The goal of each meditation session is to break the cycle of overthinking, identify recurring negative ideas and thoughts, and refocus your attention on the present moment. Over time, meditation strengthens your ability to calm your mind and manage intrusive thoughts, which can increase your resilience during stressful times.

8. Fight Against Perfectionism

There is nothing wrong with setting high standards for yourself, as long as those standards are realistic. The trouble with unrealistic standards is that they make the process of pursuing goals stressful, rather than empowering. Moreover, instead of focusing on making small, consistent progress, you might go to extreme lengths to achieve lofty goals. One of the ways to fight against perfectionism is to remind yourself that progress is better than perfection, and focus on making small adjustments to how you manage the work-life balance.

9. Disconnect From Work

After the workday is over, get into the habit of disengaging from work. This means putting your laptop in the car, closing all work apps, and putting your work phone on "silent." If you have grown accustomed to working around the clock (this is especially true for female entrepreneurs), set reasonable work hours, and about 30–45 minutes before your workday is over, start to mentally prepare to disconnect. For example, you might start cleaning your workspace, responding to the last batch of emails, or preparing your work tasks for tomorrow.

10. Take Time Off Work

When was the last time you took leave? An immediate way to combat burnout is to take some time off work and focus on other non-work-related interests and hobbies. I understand that taking leave is not easy, especially if you are a high performer handling several work projects. Therefore, it is advised that you book your time off well in advance to avoid short notice breaks. Take out your work calendar and look at the next three months. How many days off have you booked? When is your next booked time off? Start planning your leave right now, so that it doesn't conflict with your work commitments.

11. Seek Support

A strong network of friends and family can offer you emotional support during stressful times. If you live far away from friends and family, scheduling regular virtual calls and video chats can be a great way to stay connected. You may also want to reflect on how much time you invest in your non-work relationships and be intentional about showing up for others, attending social gatherings, and having constructive conversations about life and wellness with your social group.

12. Identify Your Coping Mechanisms

Be mindful of how you respond to stressful situations throughout the day. For the first few weeks, note what behaviors you turn to when you are feeling overwhelmed, anxious, or cynical. You can also reflect on which coping mechanisms yield positive and negative results, and experiment with alternative strategies to replace negative coping mechanisms. It is important to have fun with this and see it as a way to gain deeper awareness about how you manage stress.

Note that your short-term burnout recovery plan doesn't need to include all of these suggestions. For example, eating right and getting into a consistent sleeping routine could be your main priorities right now, but later on, learning a great stress management technique like meditation might be top on your priority list.

Moreover, be careful not to overwhelm yourself with too many coping strategies, to the extent of procrastinating or feeling anxious. You will experience a significant improvement in your overall well-being by committing to even one of these coping strategies.

As soon as you feel that the burnout symptoms have stabilized, you can apply the following steps to help you break the cycle of burnout for good!

STEP 2

Reset the Dial in Your Life—Relax! The Building Won't Collapse Without You

> *The direction you choose to face*
> *determines whether you're standing at the end*
> *or the beginning of a road.*
>
> Richelle E. Goodrich

The Clean Out

Before making any significant changes to your life, it is important to assess where you are and where you need to be. During this self-assessment, you will discover aspects of your life that need to be adjusted in order to regain a sense of order and make progress.

I like to call this stage the clean-out.

Getting rid of habits that no longer serve you is not always an enjoyable process. In most cases, it requires you to take an honest look at yourself, ask some tough questions, and be willing to change how you think and live your life.

For instance, a third of your workday may be spent unproductively on tasks or habits that don't provide the best return on investment. We call these time and energy wasters. Although everybody will identify different time and energy wasters in their work schedule, some of the common ones include unnecessary meetings, performing tasks that aren't a priority, and "going with the flow" and not creating structure in your day. Other habits that can also be time wasters include being indecisive, multitasking, worrying about factors outside of your control, getting distracted on social media, and not being clear on what you need to do each day.

Many years ago, there was a show on TV called *Clean House*. The host, along with a builder and interior designer, would visit the home of a chronic hoarder whose habit of collecting items was negatively impacting their life. Before the team could clean and renovate the house, they had to first declutter the space, which meant selling a good portion of the homeowner's possessions.

I watched several episodes of this show, and not once did I witness a homeowner who was happy to sell their unused belongings—even possessions that were noticeably in bad condition. Even though they were determined to live a clutter-free life, breaking old habits was tough!

During the clean-out, there will be moments when you second-guess your decision to change your workplace habits. Despite how worn out and miserable you might feel, embracing new changes is uncomfortable. You have functioned in a toxic manner for so long that even positive adjustments need some getting used to. The best way to survive the clean-out is to remind yourself of the big "WHY": Why did you decide to address your feelings of burnout in the first place? What is the motivating force driving this desire for change?

Trust that the small and big steps you are taking to reset your life and improve your relationship with work will pay off in the end. You will be able to live a lifestyle that aligns with your core values and supports your physical, mental, and emotional needs. The sacrifices you make to combat work-related stress will be worth it.

Three Types of Burnout Recovery

Recovery from burnout will look different for each woman. Why? Because we each have different triggers, stress tolerance levels, and coping strategies. When you have identified the cause of your burnout, you can choose between three types of recovery, which are:

1. External Burnout Recovery

The first type of recovery focuses on healing physical manifestations of burnout, such as fatigue, migraines, digestive issues, or poor sleep. Some of the techniques you might use include cutting out caffeine and drinking more water, eating whole and natural foods and fibers, increasing physical activity, and creating a structured sleeping schedule. The type of people you can reach out to for support are gym instructors, nutritionists, and naturopathic/holistic doctors.

2. Internal Burnout Recovery

The second type of recovery looks inward and seeks to address psychological manifestations of burnout, such as stress, anxiety, and imposter syndrome. There are quite a number of therapies that can help you deal with emotional distress, like cognitive behavioral therapy (CBT), mindfulness, and talk therapy. Examples of exercises you can practice at home include reframing negative thoughts, practicing breathing techniques, meditation, and journaling. The type of people you can reach out to for support are trained therapists, counselors, social workers, mentors, or life coaches.

3. Daily Burnout Recovery

The third type of recovery focuses on fighting burnout by making small adjustments to your daily routine. This is often the go-to recovery for working women who may be looking to make gradual lifestyle changes, without interfering with their professional and personal obligations. For example, you may not be able to reduce the amount of workload right now, but learning effective time management skills can alleviate the stress of having a lot on your plate. The type of people who can support you during recovery are work colleagues, particularly the human resources (HR) department or employee welfare unit, and close friends and family.

What is important to understand about burnout recovery is that it isn't a miracle cure. The current challenges you face in your personal and professional life won't suddenly disappear; and, in some cases, they might never go away. However, committing to recovery helps you learn new ways of responding to stress-inducing situations, so you can remain resilient during difficult times.

Identify Perfectionism

Do you know what the secret killer of productivity is? Perfectionism. We can define perfectionism as upholding unrealistically high standards for ourselves and others. On the surface, it may seem like a good source of motivation. After all, who doesn't want to aim to be the best at what they do? But more often than not, these high standards cause you to become extremely self-critical.

In the workplace, perfectionism can be self-destructive. Instead of seizing opportunities and taking calculated risks that lead to career advancement, you may doubt your competence or act overly cautious. Hewlett-Packard completed an internal study investigating the differences in attitudes toward job applications for male and female employees.

The study found that women were more likely to apply for a job when they matched 100% of the job specs, whereas men were willing to apply for a job when they met 60% of the job specs (Wynter, 2018). This finding tells us that women are comparatively more self-conscious about their work performance to the extent of delaying their own promotions.

It is difficult to speak about perfectionism without sounding like you are bashing top achievers. Perhaps this is due to the word "perfectionism" being seen as the pursuit of excellence, but there is a difference between the two. Perfectionism is striving for a goal post that keeps on changing the closer you get to it, whereas pursuing excellence is about focusing on incremental development so you can work more efficiently than you did a few months or years ago.

You can also tell the difference between perfectionism and the pursuit of excellence by how they make you feel. When you are a perfectionist, nothing that you do ever seems like enough because the work standards you set are so high that you always fall short. This is the reason why perfectionism leads to burnout—the amount of commitment shown to your work is never enough.

On the other hand, pursuing excellence feels incredibly rewarding because every small win seems like a major leap in the right direction. Plus, you are more energized by the holistic improvements in your life, such as getting more sleep and living an active lifestyle, instead of only focusing on career growth.

Overcoming perfectionism has a lot to do with adjusting your mindset. You must be willing to rethink your standards and the value you place on your work. Whenever your work becomes more important than your health or intimate relationships, you have a problem. Yes, by all means, go ahead and pursue those amazing work goals. However, do it at your own pace, according to your own standards, and not at the expense of your physical, mental, and emotional well-being. Below are three strategies that you can use to practice overcoming perfectionism:

1. Redefine Your Standards

The main trigger of perfectionism is having excessively high expectations of yourself and others. While it is good to set standards that stretch you, they shouldn't overwhelm you. For example, the best type of goals are said to be S.MA.R.T goals because they are specific, measurable, achievable, relevant, and time-based. They offer enough of a challenge to get you to think and move differently, but they are still within your capacity to achieve. Keep your standards aspirational without stepping over your limits.

2. Challenge the Inner Critic

The battle with perfectionism is fought and won in the mind. You may not always realize it, but there is constantly an internal dialogue playing in your head. Your mind brings forward ideas that reinforce beliefs about who you are and how you interact with the world around you. If you identify as a perfectionist, it is common to have self-limiting beliefs about yourself, such as not being qualified for your role or not feeling good about yourself when you don't receive validation from others.

These self-limiting beliefs must be identified and challenged whenever they arise. If you are able to catch the belief as it arises in your head, pause your thinking and ask yourself questions about its validity. Below are examples of questions to ask:

- What belief is being presented?
- What assumption is being made?
- Is there any evidence of this belief being true?
- Is this belief based on black-or-white thinking when life is more complicated?
- Does this belief consider all the evidence, or based on

my opinions?

- Did this belief come from me, or was it influenced by someone else's thoughts?
- Is this belief a true reflection of what is happening now, or could I be triggered?

The inner critical voice can teach you a lot about yourself. Whenever those negative, self-doubting thoughts appear, take the time to listen and respond with compassion. Learn about where they come from and what they reveal about your current psychological well-being. You can even journal about recurring self-limiting beliefs and record the journey of confronting and challenging them.

3. Avoid Over-Identifying With Your Work

Yes. Finding purpose at work is important. Heck, even finding purpose in your work is wonderful. Although when your role at work becomes the only role in your life that feels meaningful or makes you happy, then it can lead to overidentifying with your work.

Overidentifying with your work occurs when you find it difficult to distinguish between who you are and what you do. For example, when things are going well for you at work, you feel confident and proud of yourself, but as soon as you are placed under significant stress, you may start to question if you are fit to lead or perform your work tasks. It is important to separate your sense of self from your career so that whether you are enjoying your job or experiencing temporary lows, your self-perception remains stable.

Recognize that you are one person with a personal and professional life, but that you play different roles in each of these aspects of your life. Who you are at work should be distinct from who you are at home or with your friends. Additionally, the struggles you face at work should be kept within the confines of your office and not leak over to your personal life.

The Check-In

The purpose of the clean-out is to increase self-awareness, so you can get behind your thoughts, emotions, and actions. The ability to introspect is referred to as the check-in. During the process of burnout recovery, it is important to check in with yourself before implementing any changes. Why? Because understanding your personal and professional needs helps you combat the source of burnout, rather than merely softening the symptoms.

You might be wondering what exactly "checking in with yourself" looks like. The answer is that it can look different for each person. For example, some women enjoy having audible conversations with themselves and asking questions like "How am I feeling right now?" and "Is there anything missing at this moment?" This practice might creep out other women who prefer more structured methods of introspection, like journaling.

The emphasis here is on finding methods that feel comfortable to you because essentially, check-ins will become a daily (and sometimes hourly) occurrence as you go through the process of overcoming burnout. Below are a few examples of ways that you can check in with yourself.

Journaling

Writing your thoughts on paper, a practice known as journaling has similar effects to talk therapy. The only difference of course is that you are not speaking to a therapist, but instead reflecting on your life circumstances as though you were an outsider looking in.

Journaling can also help you keep track of your thought patterns or behaviors so you can measure your progress over time. All you need to get started with journaling is a pen, notebook, and a few journal prompts. Here are some prompts to get you writing about your life outside of work:

- How do you like to spend your free time?
- Describe your ideal day.
- What are you scared of, and why?
- Write about your favorite childhood memory.
- What makes you smile?

The objective of journal prompts is to make it easier to share uncomfortable truths or explore aspects of your daily life that you rarely think about. Feel free to write as much or as little as you wish, and refer back to your journal entries on a regular basis.

Meditation

Have you ever tried listening to your thoughts when your mind is frantic? It can feel as loud and chaotic as the streets of Lagos or New York. It's no wonder that you find it difficult to reason with yourself during stressful work situations—your mind is moving at 120 mph and nothing you say to yourself sticks long enough to change your mood or behaviors.

Meditation is a technique that trains your mind to slow down and relax. Even though you are supposed to practice meditation when you are calm, it creates new connections in your brain that adjust your response to triggering work and life circumstances. For example, the more regularly you meditate, the easier it becomes to identify physical signs of uneasiness, like having heart palpitations or feeling restless. This gives you an opportunity to diffuse a situation before it becomes a full-blown trigger.

If you are trying meditation for the first time, I would recommend finding a quiet spot at home or in the office where you can retreat whenever you desire to calm your mind. It can also serve as a "safe place" that you can go to when you need a few minutes to just breathe. Remove all distractions nearby and sit in a comfortable position. Set a timer for five minutes (or longer if you like), and close your eyes.

Center yourself by focusing on your breathing and noticing any changes. Whenever you feel your mind wandering off, simply redirect your focus back to your breathing. Once you have mastered this beginner-friendly meditation, you can explore other types of meditation that induce relaxation and increase self-awareness.

Gratitude

There is no doubt that our lifestyles have become busier. For many women, maintaining a job is not the only responsibility in their lives. There is family, children, household maintenance, financial investments, education, and so much more! Thinking about all of your responsibilities can be emotionally exhausting, but even worse than this, it can cause you to lose sight of what's going right in your life.

I have observed this many times with myself. Preoccupying my mind with long lists of tasks and constant reminders of responsibilities has caused me to feel like I am running out of time, or as though I am not strong enough to manage my life. It was only when I shifted my focus to the progress I was making in each area of my life, that I felt a sense of relief. Gratitude is the ability to appreciate the goodness present in every moment. Even in the worst of situations, there is something that you can stop and be thankful for. The reason it may not always feel like this is because of where your attention is focused.

You need to be deliberate in looking for positive evidence that things are okay, or that they will be okay. When you do this, your mind shifts from obsessing over what isn't working to appreciating what is.

Continuous Learning

There is a myth that as you get older, your brain power decreases, and therefore you can't easily absorb new information. Neuroscientists have debunked this myth by showing evidence of the brain forming new neural pathways well into late adulthood (WBT Systems, n.d.). This concept is known as neuroplasticity. Continuous learning helps you check in with your personal development. It ensures that at the end of each year, you can look back and say, "Wow, I can't believe how much I have grown!"

Learning new skills, hobbies, or knowledge adjusts your thinking, which also adjusts how you navigate work, parenting, financial planning, and other important areas of your life. The reality is that you cannot move ahead to the next stage of your life, leaning on the wisdom that got you where you are. You need to be open to learning new beliefs and habits that will stretch you enough to reach the next stage.

Note that what you learn and how you learn doesn't need to be formal. For instance, if you have already been through university, the last thing you want is to go back to that particular style of learning. There are other engaging ways of learning, such as listening to a podcast, reading a book, enrolling in an online course, or attending a training seminar. Explore your options and find fun learning tools!

Self-Care

Many of us are introduced to self-care through commercials advertising the latest beauty treatments or kitchen gadgets. It's a pity that such a vital practice of taking care of the mind, body, and soul has been hijacked by consumerist culture. The truth is that self-care has a lot more to do with how well you respond to your needs than how much you spend on yourself. Responding to your needs can take on different forms, such as picking up on triggers and responding with decisive action, creating healthy boundaries, scheduling time for relaxation, and so on.

As women, we are often conditioned to make sure everyone else is okay before we can respond to our own needs. Self-care may sound selfish or indulgent because we are not used to taking priority in our own lives. I love the analogy of the flight safety protocol in explaining the importance of self-care. Before a flight takes off, the host or hostess will conduct a safety briefing. One of the instructions they give is to fit a mask over your face before assisting other passengers in the event of a loss of cabin pressure.

Self-care is very much like fitting your mask first. It isn't out of selfishness that you prioritize your physical, mental, and emotional needs—it is a matter of survival! Plus, when you extend yourself from a place of being stable and balanced, you are able to assist others without feeling burned out or taken for granted.

There isn't a one-size-fits-all approach to practicing self-care because it is ultimately about responding to your needs through activities that you love. If you don't already have a list of go-to self-care activities, here are a few suggestions to consider below.

Self-Care for the Mind

- Listen to a guided meditation.
- Unfollow triggering social media accounts.
- Declutter your living space and workspace.
- Accomplish a small goal.
- Create a vision board.
- Learn a new skill.

Self-Care for the Body

- Practice a deep breathing exercise.
- Go for a relaxing walk.
- Prepare a healthy meal.
- Get on a consistent sleeping schedule.

- Get at least 10 minutes of natural sunlight.
- Attend a fun fitness class.

Self-Care for the Soul

- Do a random act of kindness.
- Journal your thoughts and feelings.
- Take yourself on a date.
- Review your list of short and long-term goals.
- Play with your children or pets.
- Plan a vacation.
- Remove toxic relationships from your life.

Besides activities, self-care can also be taking a five-minute break and asking yourself questions about your physical, mental, and emotional state. Below are a few questions that you can write on flash cards and keep in your car, office desk, or handbag:

- How am I feeling today?
- What does my body need right now?
- How can I be gentler with myself?
- Do I feel physically and emotionally safe?
- What have I done today to feel good about myself?
- Who has been my source of strength today?

There will be times when life happens and you either forget or can't seem to find the time to perform a check-in. To prevent these situations from happening, you can get into the habit of scheduling check-ins in your diary. If doing a check-in on a daily basis is too much, you can schedule one per week or one every two weeks. Be specific about where the check-in will take place, how long it will be, and what resources you will need on hand. The more prepared you are, the fewer barriers you will face when the time comes.

Beyond Work-Life Balance

Talitha is a 32-year-old mother of two beautiful boys, both under the age of five. After taking a few years off work to raise her boys, she decided to start a small business. On the outside, it  looks like she has it all: She is a stay-at-home mother and a budding entrepreneur at the same time.

However, under the supermom disguise, Talitha often feels overwhelmed by the different hats she needs to wear. Most of it is self-inflicted pressure to be the best mom while being a respectable business owner. When she can't excel in one area, she feels a wave of anxiety coming over her, as though the work-life structures she has spent a few years rebuilding are about to collapse. All of this anxiety puts a strain on her physical and emotional well-being, and makes it difficult for her to be a present mother and boss.

The concept of work-life balance gained popularity around the '80s when women traditional stay-at-home moms were entering the workforce in numbers. Having never participated in the corporate environment before, these women felt the pressure to "fit in" the workplace by adopting common work practices, without neglecting their roles as spouses and mothers. The concept was taken literally to mean that half of a woman's time needed to be invested in work-related activities and the other half had to be invested in taking care of home life.

There is no doubt in my mind that the concept of a work-life balance was supposed to help working women balance their increasing responsibilities. However, over the years, this concept has created an unrealistic expectation for women to "have it all" and "do it all." All over magazines and social media, we see portrayals of supermoms who work upwards of 60 hours a week and never miss a parent-teacher meeting. A working mother who is struggling to give 100% to her career or family responsibilities might regard these supermoms as the ideal and feel inferior in comparison to them. For instance, they might think, "If she can build an empire and raise five children on her own, why can't I?"

What makes the concept of the work-life balance harmful is that it suggests you can invest equal time and effort in various areas of your life, such as being career-focused and a devoted parent simultaneously. If you had unlimited energy and more than 24 hours in a day, maybe this would be possible. But since you can only be in one place at any given moment, and have a limited amount of time available for any given task, striking a balance means doing a little each day to respond to several needs. For example, your life can be split into different domains, namely:

- career
- family life
- physical, mental, and emotional health
- social life
- spirituality

It is impossible to give 100% to each domain because you have a finite amount of energy. Instead, you can divide your time and energy among the domains, investing more in the areas that matter most in this season of your life. For example, there are some women who don't have families yet and can invest more time and energy into other domains, like their social lives.

When your attention is distributed proportionately to various domains in your life, taking care of your needs becomes a lot less daunting. You are aware of how much importance is given to each area of your life and won't feel guilty if you are not progressing as quickly in other areas. In other words, you take control of your responsibilities rather than allowing your responsibilities to overwhelm you. It also means that instead of referring to a work-life balance, you ultimately create a work-family-health-social-spirituality balance.

Your Time Out Action Plan

Striking a balance is also about taking the need for rest seriously. The energy that you expend during the day has to come from somewhere. It isn't realistic to think that you can work long hours—and even on some weekends—without taking time off to replenish the energy you have spent.

With all this said, I can relate to the reluctance many professionals feel to take time off. It isn't that we don't sense the physical and mental exhaustion, but that we fear missing out on important decisions or having to catch up on excessive work when we get back. Another reason for the reluctance to take time off is being unable to detach mentally from work. This has become increasingly harder post-pandemic, as many people work from home. There is never really a sense that the workday is over because the lines between private and professional space have been blurred.

But taking time off can work to your advantage, especially if you want to successfully climb the corporate ladder. It gives your brain an opportunity to recharge and focus on non-work activities, like practicing self-care, exploring hobbies and side interests, or prioritizing your emotional well-being. When you return to work, you experience a greater sense of mental clarity and flow of creativity, which positively affects your levels of productivity.

Time off can also be a great way to maintain a healthy relationship with work. Even if you love what you do, prioritizing rest and having a life outside of work ensures that you don't overwork yourself. You can create your own time-out action plan to schedule your time off in advance. Periodically (every quarter or bi-annually), you can revisit your plan and make sure you are taking enough rest in between your busy work schedule.

Since taking time off is not something you can do on a whim, you can schedule your leave days in advance. A time-out action plan is a checklist that you can refer to whenever you are thinking about requesting time off. It considers all of the necessary people and details that need to be dealt with to ensure that you enjoy guilt-free time away from work. Below is an outline of the checklist:

1. Is It Paid or Unpaid Time Out?

Before you request time off, check to see if you qualify for paid or unpaid leave. Depending on your company's policy, you may have several days of paid leave that accumulate on a monthly basis.

2. Which Time of the Month or Year?

While you deserve a break from work, there are certain times of the month or year when your company (or industry at large) is busiest, and taking time off might jeopardize the performance of your team. Try to schedule your leave around busy seasons, so that your absence does not create frustration at work.

3. Have You Caught Up With Your Work?

Another awkward time to take a break from work is when you have a lot of work piled up. Essentially, this ends up being one of the main reasons why people don't request time off. If possible, do your best to stay on top of deadlines and avoid taking on more work projects near the time when you are planning to take leave.

4. Have You Communicated With Your Team?

If you are part of a team, you may want to let your coworkers know, since this is likely to impact work being redistributed among them. Discuss how many days off you are thinking of taking, why taking a break is important for you, and what work tasks they might need to take over in your absence.

Make sure to revisit your time-out action plan every few months, planning ahead to take periodic breaks gives you something to look forward to and helps avoid the need to take a break only when you are at the point of breaking.

STEP 3

Invoke Your Inner Warrior—Reignite Your Passion for Your Career Goals

*Success is liking yourself, liking what you do,
and liking how you do it.*

Maya Angelou

Finding Your Groove at Work

A colleague once told me about her career journey, which began many years before she actually started working. The earliest memory she had of wanting to join the science, technology, engineering, and mathematics (STEM) fields was during a fight with her older brother, at the age of 16.

She told him that she was thinking of studying engineering at university. He laughed in her face and said, "To get into that field, you will need to work 10 times harder than average students. I don't think you have what it takes." Fortunately, her high school marks proved otherwise, and she was accepted into her university of choice to study engineering. But not long after she had settled in, my colleague heard similar mocking messages from one of her male lecturers, and again from talent recruiters.

Despite the doom and gloom that those few people predicted, she graduated from university and got a job within the engineering space. Finally, the negative chitter-chatter in her ear had been silenced, but now she had a different kind of critic—the inner critic who lived inside her head and replayed all of her inherited fears and doubts. Instead of silencing the haters, her biggest challenge became silencing her own negative self-talk, so she could fully take in the opportunity that was in front of her.

Even though my career journey was different, I can relate to how my colleague felt struggling to find her place in the corporate world. I remember having to deal with the inner critic too, and feeling like I didn't belong in my work environment. Slowly, I started to feel the pressure to be the poster child for a woman of color climbing up the ranks and achieving incredible goals. I felt that if I wanted to be heard and respected, I had to work harder and longer to prove my worth. I thought that my actions would guarantee career success and improve my visibility at work.

This, however, came at a price. It took a strain on my physical, mental, and emotional being. I was tired all the time and lost some of what I regarded as my natural traits. I was becoming less patient and empathetic, and in some cases even coming across as angry.

Reality sunk in when I discovered that changing who I was wouldn't lead to career success; it would only lead to burnout and a heap of insecurities that I would later need to address. I was angry at myself and the patriarchal system because I couldn't figure out how to beat the system without becoming the thing I hated the most. I was left wondering if I needed to give my career up altogether, or just suck it up.

I was trying to do and be all to everyone while staying true to my values. I had not learned how to influence more to get the same results with less work and no burnout. I was guilty of what is sometimes referred to as doing the office housework with no reward and all the burnout. But I eventually learned how to do both: remain empathetic, get the job done well, and avoid burnout.

To be successful at my job, I had to be authentic! I had to play to my own strengths, engage with coworkers in my own way, and communicate my thoughts and feelings honestly, without any pretense. I went through a rebranding of some sort, where I audited various aspects of my career, such as my professional image, career goals, and what success looked and felt like for me. Thereafter, I told myself that if I was going to make progress in my career, I wanted it to result from developing my own character, skills, and talents!

Has it ever dawned on you that part of the reason why you overwork is due to spending unpaid hours supporting your colleagues and picking up extra tasks that you aren't recognized or rewarded for? You don't want your team to look bad, so what do you do? Work overtime and volunteer to take on more workload, as though you don't have kids and an entire household to manage. And what about the emotional labor that you do during and outside of work hours? You feel responsible for checking in with your team and making sure they are motivated, all the while you are drained, underappreciated, and in need of some TLC, too.

The truth is, you cannot convincingly do your job when your tank is running low. Invoking your inner warrior at work is about rediscovering who you are, why you love the job you do, and how you can show up more authentically—so that you don't end up losing yourself in your job.

How to Define Success on Your Own Terms

During the process of recovering from burnout, you are presented with a unique opportunity to define success on your own terms. You have a choice about how you get back up and approach your life moving forward.

It is so easy to lose yourself in the pursuit of your career goals that you forget to look at success holistically, considering the big picture of the lifestyle you desire. Society's expectations of women always tempt them to have an "either-or" approach to designing their lifestyles.

For example, women are told that they can either be working women or stay-at-home mothers. Or they can either focus on climbing the corporate ladder or start their own business. This "either-or" approach causes women to compromise on what makes them genuinely happy and settle on one aspect of success that doesn't make them feel completely satisfied.

The truth is, success is about achieving balance in your life so that you have the time to engage in different interests, activities, and responsibilities that provide satisfaction. However, striking a good balance is not always possible, and there are seasons in life where making small progress or just getting through each day makes you successful!

The definition of success should always be specific to your current needs, goals, and desires in life. That can change at different seasons or stages in your life, but that's okay. Focus on what success means to you now. There are three strategies that can help you begin to reflect on what success looks and feels like for you. These strategies include:

1. Reestablish Your Standards

Going into the workplace, you had a set of standards that informed your attitude toward work. These standards were most likely influenced by what you read or were told about the corporate environment. They could have also been influenced by family or societal expectations of women in the workplace. Both the success stories and the horror stories shaped what you believed was the best way to approach your job.

Some of these standards served you well, but there are others that have compromised your well-being, or negatively shaped how you perceive yourself as a working woman. When defining career success in your own terms, it's important to audit these standards and decide what YOU expect from yourself at work. Remember, the time, energy, and effort to do your job effectively need to come from you. Therefore, your standards are designed to give you a healthy push in the right direction, while ensuring that you don't overextend yourself.

Consider what values are most important to uphold at work. For instance, do you care about effective time management? Or collaborating with others? You can also think about the ideal work relationships with coworkers, such as how you expect to be treated and how you manage conflict. It is also crucial to define what "hard work" means for you, how much of a priority it is, and the kind of expectations you can create to establish a habit of working hard.

2. See Success as Being More Than One Ideal

Due to the lack of representation of women throughout organizational hierarchies, it's common to find one type of success represented at work, such as the woman who is on the board of directors, or the few women who are senior managers. But the truth of the matter is that career success is more than climbing up the ranks and being promoted into senior positions. Other forms of career success could be becoming an expert in your field, mentoring young people, achieving financial stability, or starting your own side business.

The broad definition of success is the completion of an achievement. With this definition, you have a lot of room to succeed on your own terms. Your success doesn't even need to be defined by your job. You can find other aspects of your life that bring the most fulfillment and brainstorm ideas on how you can turn those interests into meaningful goals.

Moreover, accept the fact that not everyone will share the same desires as you, and vice versa. If you don't see other women jumping at the opportunity to start a side hustle, it doesn't mean that you shouldn't give it a shot! Depending on your personal and professional network, as well as your exposure and environment, you may be the only woman who aspires to certain goals. Be careful not to seek validation from your peers, or feel discouraged when your dreams are mocked. Not everyone is moving on the same path as you, and that is okay!

3. Be Willing to Do the Work

Doing hard work is something that we cannot avoid. Many people mistakenly believe that the reason they are burned out is that they have invested a lot of time into their careers, but that isn't the case. The real reason people feel burned out is that they overextend themselves and not necessarily that they work hard.

To be successful at anything in life, you will need to discover what is meaningful to you. The good news though is that once you find meaningful work, the hard work becomes enjoyable. This is often called "being in the zone" or "entering the flow state," where you are so focused on the work you are doing that you lose track of time. But you will need to strike a balance though, because while finding meaningful work can be enjoyable, doing too much can bring you back into the burnout cycle.

Also, note that hard work has nothing to do with perfection. You don't need to measure your progress based on productivity metrics, unless, of course, you are doing it as a way to motivate yourself. Nonetheless, be careful not to allow your mind to bully your body. Taking time off work, engaging in non-work activities, socializing with friends, and getting enough sleep can help you maintain the momentum of hard work for a long period of time.

Create a New Template

It is predicted that one-third of our lives are spent at work. This shows just how important having a career is. However, we often overestimate the importance of work and make it the center of our lives—the sole activity from where we derive our sense of purpose. Our lives were never supposed to revolve around any single area, but rather allow for personal development in several different areas.

Don't get me wrong, I do believe that having a career and being dedicated to your work can be fulfilling and respond to many of your emotional and intellectual needs. Your work can be a great way to live out your life's values, earn a living, contribute to the greater good of others, and increase your self-confidence. All of these benefits are wonderful, and they enhance your quality of life. But when your main purpose in life is to achieve career goals, other aspects of your life are neglected, and what started out as a passion ends up being the source of all your stress.

To prevent or fight burnout, you need to create a new template for living a meaningful life. This template must include several aspects of your life that bring a sense of satisfaction and allow for personal development. Work cannot be the only thing that makes you happy or feel accomplished; it cannot shape your identity, replace your family, or be the only area of your life where you set goals. The purpose of creating a new template is to remind yourself that life is so much more than any single ambition—it is a journey of rediscovering yourself, repeatedly, through different aspirations, interests, and relationships.

There are five steps that you can follow to create a new template for your life and achieve more balance.

Step 1: Create a Vision

Consider each important area of your life and the "ideal" you hope to achieve. Imagine that you manifested the dream career, dream health, dream relationships, and so on. Create steps to achieve these ideals, starting from where you are now. The more detailed your vision is, the easier it will be to plan your action steps for each area of your life.

For example, if improving your health is part of the vision, some of the action steps to achieve that ideal would be cutting back on sugar and processed foods, increasing your physical activity by 20% per week, and getting at least six uninterrupted hours of sleep every night. Your career ideal might be running your own passive business. Some of the action steps you may need to take include studying a business course, finding a mentor, saving at least 15% of your salary toward start-up capital, etc.

Step 2: Identify Your Core Values

By reflecting on your dream life, you can start to pick up on some of your core values. We can define core values as the standards that make up the foundation of your life. In other words, in order to feel fulfilled, it is important that your core values are reflected in your career, health, lifestyle, and relationships.

You can identify core values by thinking about the things that motivate you. For example, in the area of work, you may be motivated by interacting with colleagues or having one-on-one time with customers. This could mean that you value building meaningful relationships. In other areas of your life, let's say your finances, you may be motivated by sticking to a budget and increasing your savings. This could mean that you value financial security. Another great way to identify your core values is by taking the https://casaa.unm.edu/inst/Personal%20Values%20Card%20Sort.pdf exercise, so you can find out what is truly important to you!

Step 3: Bridge the Gap

Now that you are aware of what you desire to achieve and what your core values are, it's time to bridge the gap! Conduct a self-assessment for each area of your life, reflecting on the current state and any strengths or weaknesses you can observe. When doing this exercise, openness (rather than self-criticism) will give you the best results. The aim is to identify specific aspects of your life that must be improved in order to live out your core values and achieve your wildest dreams.

It might even be useful to rate each area of your life on a scale of 1–10 (1 being unsatisfactory and 10 being immensely satisfying) based on how aligned they are with your core values. Every few months, review your ratings and make the necessary adjustments.

Step 4: Create an Action Plan

The fun part of creating a new life template is to brainstorm daily behaviors (that will hopefully become habits), which will help you achieve the action steps highlighted in the first step. These daily behaviors must be small enough to practice without a lot of physical or mental exertion, and they should also easily integrate into your current lifestyle. The more natural and comfortable it feels performing these behaviors, the more likely you are to stick with them!

For example, if you desire to be promoted to an executive position at work (vision) and one of the steps to achieve that is to further your training (action step), you can conduct research on various educational institutions and courses for 30 minutes. This behavior is small enough to practice without putting a lot of strain on yourself and it integrates perfectly into your current lifestyle.

Step 5: Adjust the Plan Accordingly

Your new template should serve as a guideline that supports your dreams, not one that applies pressure to your life. There will be times when you derail from the action plan and revert to old habits. This is okay. As soon as you recognize that you are moving in the wrong direction, assess how you got there and what needs to change in order not to lose sight of your dreams again.

Your plan should also complement your lifestyle, instead of placing you so far out of your comfort zone that staying committed is difficult. This means that you should regularly adjust your daily behaviors so that they match the current demands of your life. For instance, during busy months at work, you may not be able to attend the gym after work due to feeling tired. One of the adjustments you could make is waking up 30 minutes earlier in the morning and doing an at-home moderate workout. To know when you need to make adjustments, monitor changes to your availability and update your action plan accordingly.

Let Your Inner Warrior Speak Up

So far, I have touched on the different ways you can invoke your inner warrior, such as redefining career success and creating a new template for your life that considers a wide variety of your needs. However, once the inner warrior has been invoked, the next reasonable step is to find ways of displaying her strength confidently. The inner warrior is not a troublemaker who emerges to create conflict or division at work. Her purpose is to be your advocate and ensure that you ask for what you need to support you. Some women don't have difficulties asking for what they need, but others need guidance articulating their values, and clarifying what is important to them.

It is still difficult for companies to accept that a major reason some of their employees are constantly sick, stressed out, or resigning after only a few months has to do with the systemic distribution of work that places a severe strain on workers. The inner warrior thrives in situations where your physical, mental, and emotional needs are at risk of being compromised. Think of it as the part of you that is fiercely protective and compassionate about your well-being. When you are feeling overwhelmed with work responsibilities and need support, you can allow the inner warrior to speak up for you!

However, before you do that, there are a few questions you will need to think about, such as:

- What isn't currently working?
- What boundary has been crossed?
- What physical, mental, and emotional needs are being neglected?
- In a sentence, what am I asking for?
- What solutions could I propose?

It is common to find women who are feeling burned out, but haven't yet identified their triggers or analyzed the situation enough to figure out what they want. When they approach their managers, they come across as being confused or unprepared. Besides the inability to articulate the kind of support they need; another barrier could be a lack of confidence. For instance, they may be able to figure out what they want but feel afraid to make the request.

Negotiating a salary increase is one of the many fears women have. They don't want to be penalized or seen unfavorably when asking for a raise. This fear affects their confidence going into the negotiations, which makes it harder to be persuasive. A study by McKinsey & Company found that women struggle to quantify what they want, like being able to ask for a specific amount of money when negotiating a raise (Become Team, 2021). As a result of this ambiguity, they were less likely to receive an amount close to what they had in mind.

Knowing how to ask for support is just as important as realizing that you need support. Once you have identified work-related issues preventing you from effectively doing your job, the inner warrior can step forward and do the bidding on your behalf. Summoning the courage to clearly communicate what you need can be achieved by following these tips:

- **Examine your true intentions.** It is crucial to rule out ego needs when making requests, such as asking for leniency with deadlines, because that's what you saw your peers doing. When your "why for making a request is not rooted in a genuine need, the solution will never feel satisfying. In other words, your ego will want more and more, regardless of the compromises that have been reached.

- **Take ownership of your shortcomings.** Another bitter pill to swallow is admitting your own shortcomings that have contributed to the build-up of stress at work. For example, your time management skills might need more fine-tuning, or maybe your communication boundaries (such as how you resolve conflict) are weak and you struggle to stand up for yourself. Owning your shortcomings allows you to find ways of being part of the solution, rather than believing that the solution is someone else's responsibility.

- **Present a clear vision.** One of the ways to be more convincing when asking for a raise or approaching other tough conversations is to present your career vision. The goal of your vision is to map out where you want to go and the various milestones you will need to achieve along the way. Presenting your vision during a conversation gives your manager an opportunity to see where they can support you and how much support they give.

- **Link your request to contributions and tangible results.** Getting your needs met is important to you, but have you thought about what is important to the leadership in your company? What would make them believe you are deserving of the request? When it comes down to it, business performance is what companies care about the most. When making your request, be forthcoming about the contributions you have made to the success of your team or company at large. Be specific, mentioning recent reports, metrics, and milestones.

- **Explain what you bring to the table (don't assume they already know).** When advocating for yourself, there is no room for modesty because it can be perceived as being unsure of yourself. Spend time going through your accomplishments, so that your manager is aware of the work you have put in, which makes you deserving of recognition or a promotion. If you can get feedback from your work team, and maybe a few loyal customers, this can also help to build your case!

- **Present a win-win situation.** Before giving your manager an opportunity to respond, end your negotiation by presenting a few solutions. Not only will this show that you have done your homework and taken your request seriously, but it will also give you a chance to show the other party how they can benefit too. Empathize with the challenges they might be faced with and think of solutions that would be ideal for both of you. For example, working from home will make parenting less stressful because you are able to achieve more harmony with your responsibilities. This means more energy and fewer interruptions when it comes to performing your work.

I cannot guarantee that your request for support will be welcomed. However, what I can say is that learning to speak up for yourself can reduce the number of uncomfortable moments you experience at work, which take a toll on your health. Plus, when you practice assertively communicating your needs, you can gain deeper trust in your capabilities and start behaving like someone who knows their worth! This can be such an empowering realization that positively shifts your mindset from victim to fierce warrior.

To Quit or Not to Quit?

Making an effort to speak up for yourself at work can significantly improve your working conditions. However, there is a possibility that regardless of your many attempts to improve your working conditions, the passion for your job cannot be reignited. Please understand that this is natural and not something you should feel guilty about. Don't allow the inner critic to make you think less of yourself for thinking about resigning.

If the desire to quit is on your mind, you have probably thought about it before and maybe felt too scared to follow through. I'll be the first to admit that mentally checking out of my previous jobs was much easier than signing the paperwork and leaving. Back then, they didn't have a name to describe mentally checking out from work, but today it is referred to as "quiet quitting," essentially doing the bare minimum just to get by. The reason why I stayed at my previous posts longer than I should have was due to thinking about what's known as the sunken cost.

In finance, the sunken cost is a term used to describe an expense that has already been paid and cannot be recovered. Whenever I thought about quitting, my mind would calculate the many sacrifices, time spent, and energy exerted to reach my position at work. After doing this mental math, the thought of leaving made me doubtful. *How can I recover the time and effort I have already invested in getting here?* I would think to myself.

You might be having the same thoughts: *How can I justify the money I spent upskilling myself? The long hours I dedicated to climbing up the ranks?* Reflecting on the investment you have made to be in the position you are in can be enough to make you stay a little longer—especially if you still have student debt and other financial obligations to take care of. The point is that quitting is not always as easy as having an idea and immediately acting upon it.

Assuming that you have considered the sunken costs and still feel determined to go ahead with your resignation, you need to be 100% certain that leaving is the best NEXT STEP for your career. In other words, you must be able to provide evidence that your next career move is a step up from your current job. It's not wise to quit your job only to go backward in your career. If this is how you are feeling, I would advise holding on to your current job a little while longer, until you find a new position that will help you level up.

Below are a few signs that quitting your job may be the BEST option:

- **You have been in the same position for several years.** If there are very few career development opportunities at work or no set formalities on getting a raise or promotion, you might consider moving to a company that offers these perks.

- **You have lost the motivation to go to work.** While it's normal to go through periods of boredom at work, it is not a good sign to dread going to work to the point of feeling anxious or experiencing physical pain.

- **The company you work for is struggling financially.** When the company is not financially stable, you have the right to look for a more stable source of income. Signs that the company may be close to going under include being paid late or not receiving your full compensation.

- **You are not adding value.** If you are not proud of your job and cannot clearly see how you contribute to the greater prosperity of the company, then you will likely feel disconnected from your work. The indifference you have toward your job is a good sign to start looking for work elsewhere.

- **The thought of staying at the company for another year stresses you.** When going to work becomes a game of surviving each moment, it's possible that you have either lost passion for your job or that you are in a toxic work environment. The best solution is to leave without causing yourself any more harm.

But leaving your job is not always ideal. Here are a few more signs that quitting may be the WORST option:

- **You don't have a career plan.** Quitting without considering what you want to do next is not a good idea. You don't need to have another job lined up, but it's important to think about which direction you would like to take, what you need to prepare to bridge the skills gap, and how you will financially sustain yourself while in between jobs.

- **You don't have any savings.** Unless you have close friends and family who can financially support you during this brief period of transition, you need to have enough cash in your savings accounts to sustain you. Downsizing your lifestyle is a great short-term solution to cut costs, but you will need consistent income in the long-term.

- **You are just going through a rough patch.** Sometimes the sheer amount of stress that you are under can make you feel like quitting. But after carrying out your short-term burnout recovery plan and making a few adjustments to your work practices, you can regain clarity and find your source of motivation again. Be careful not to make such an important decision as quitting your job when you are emotionally distressed.

- **You haven't discussed the decision with your manager.** There should be a record of at least one occasion where you called a meeting with your manager and talked about how you are feeling. Even if one foot is already out of the door, it is worth listening to how they might be able to address your concerns.

- **You might regret leaving too soon.** You don't need to tolerate a toxic work environment, but make sure that you have exhausted all of your options before going ahead with your resignation. The last thing you want is to look back and regret not waiting a few more months to renegotiate your work obligations.

For some people, quitting their corporate job is part of a career transition from employee to employer. You may be interested in starting a small business and being your own boss. This can be an exciting stage in your career because it provides new challenges that lead to personal and professional growth. However, take note of the following points before quitting your job to run a business:

- **Determine how viable your business is.** It's not recommended to quit your job while your business is still at the conception or seed stage. This is because you haven't yet tested the idea on real customers to see if it is viable or not. Hold on to your job until your business starts making some money and you at least break even.

- **Determine a need that your business solves.** The higher the demand for your products or services, the more sustainable your business will be. Don't rush the process of doing market research and finding a big enough market gap that your business can fill.

- **Determine how involved you want to be.** There are some businesses that are built with the sole purpose of generating revenue. Those businesses are usually passive and don't require the business owners to be hands-on, meaning they don't need to quit their day jobs. However, there are other businesses built on sharing value. Business owners tend to play a more active role in the day-to-day affairs of the business to supervise the quality of work. Think about the kind of business you want to run and how much of your time it will require.

If quitting right now is not an option, due to various life circumstances, you can start planning your exit strategy.

Write down a list of all the challenges preventing you from quitting. Circle the challenges that are within your control to change, and next to each, jot down three to five actionable steps that you can take on a daily, weekly, or monthly basis to slowly turn the situation around. For example, if your student debt is preventing you from quitting your job and starting a business, perhaps you can focus on reducing your debt by paying larger installments on a monthly basis.

Hold yourself accountable to the timelines stipulated on the exit strategy—the quicker you overcome these barriers, the sooner you can quit!

STEP 4

Stand Your Ground—
No Backsies!

You're not obligated to win. You're obligated to keep trying to do the best you can every day.

Marian Wright Edelman

Making It Work for You

If you have decided to stay at your job, for whatever reason, you will need to make it work for you. Making your job work for you is about investing time in factors within your control, such as adjusting your mindset, strengthening your boundaries, and becoming a better communicator at work.

It's probably worth mentioning too that although passion gives work a sense of purpose, you don't have to be passionate about what you do to find it meaningful. For example, your current job may not align with your values, nor is it a field you intend to grow in. However, since it pays the bills and allows you to save toward your side hustle (which is connected to your purpose), your job could be considered meaningful. Whether directly, or indirectly, your job adds value to your life, so staying a little longer isn't a bad idea.

Nevertheless, you cannot ignore the toxic work culture and environment. To prevent yourself from being overburdened with work or dealing with workplace drama, you will need to have a robust strategy put in place to sustain a healthier and more assertive version of yourself. The next few sections will present some of the best ways to protect your well-being at work.

Catch the Burnout Warning Signs

Once you cross over the line and reach burnout, recovery can require a lot from you. This is why preventing burnout from happening in the first place is better than treating the many related symptoms. Plus, regardless of how you may feel about your work, you want to be seen as someone consistent and dependable, and whose behaviors are predictable and professional all of the time.

This shouldn't be taken to mean that you can't have a bad day, but when this becomes the rule and not the exception, it will start to negatively impact your mental and emotional health.

I want you to think of any thought or behavior that seeks to derail your productivity at work as an act of self-sabotage. Create a personal standard for yourself that doesn't allow any form of self-sabotage into the workplace environment. Tell yourself every morning that although work isn't always enjoyable or engaging, there is a standard of behavior you need to maintain.

Some of the early symptoms of burnout which must be detected as soon as they arise—and dealt with using the short-term recovery plan—include the following:

1. You Are Emotionally Numb

When you are healthy, you feel both pleasant and difficult emotions, and neither has the power to move you out of balance. A sign that you may be fast approaching burnout is not being bothered by anything, or feeling emotionally numb. This is often an unhealthy coping mechanism to block out stress, which ironically creates more stress because you cannot release strong emotions.

2. You Are Easily Angered

On the flip side, burnout can reduce your distress tolerance and lead to unexpected emotional triggers. Once again, this is a sign that you are overwhelmed and need to urgently make adjustments to your work practices. To monitor your degree of impulsivity, measure your emotional reaction to work-related challenges from a scale of 1–10 (1 being indifferent and 10 being catastrophic). After rating your reaction, think objectively about whether the intensity of your emotion matches the nature of the problem. For example, is an 8 out of 10 reaction for entering a disagreement with a coworker appropriate?

3. You Are Reluctant to Work With Others

Another sneaky warning sign of burnout is the desire to isolate yourself at work. Regular interactions with colleagues have become draining or lead to emotional triggers, hence you prefer working independently in your office. You may even notice that relationships outside of work have become draining, too. Conversations, meeting up, or engaging in shared interests with loved ones have started to feel like chores.

4. You Are Cynical About Work

Feeling dissatisfied with your work performance, environment, and relationships to the extent of entertaining negative thoughts is a strong sign of early burnout. Of course, nobody is positive all the time because life is certainly not perfect. But being cynical about everyday tasks and responsibilities indicates that you are overwhelmed. In the worst-case scenario, it could also be a sign of imposter syndrome, where nothing you do feels like it is enough. You constantly berate yourself and others because nothing you do feels right.

5. Your Productivity Has Lowered

The inability to maintain normal work performance can be a sign of burnout too. Generally, if you are working at a comfortable pace and the workload hasn't increased, you should be able to meet your work deadlines. Low productivity in this case could indicate that you are distracted, discouraged, and not taking care of your physical well-being, like getting enough sleep.

If you are experiencing any of these burnout warning signs, it may also be good to reassess your priorities. Figure out where most of your time and energy is being spent, and whether those tasks or work situations are worth the investment. There are five questions you can answer to determine if a task or work situation is worth your time and energy:

- Is this aligned with my values?
- What will be the likely outcome of making this a priority/not making this a priority?
- Is this contributing to my growth?
- Does this invigorate me or deplete my energy?
- What personal standard of mine does this undermine?

Create Workplace Boundaries

Another way to protect your well-being at work is to set—and enforce—clear work boundaries. The topic of boundaries usually arises when discussing healthy personal relationships; however, they are just as necessary when establishing healthy ways of relating with coworkers.

A boundary is simply a limit that protects your physical, mental, and emotional well-being. It creates a distinction between your needs and expectations from those of others and ensures that your relationships align as closely as possible with your values.

The reason boundaries are important at work is that they teach others how to approach and relate with you. Since the workplace is a professional environment, there are certain standards of communication, resolving conflict, and collaboration that must be upheld so you can work efficiently.

When you are ready to create workplace boundaries, be careful not to lean toward the extremes. In other words, avoid setting boundaries that are either too rigid or too loose. What do rigid boundaries look like? Building a wall between you and others at work, so that they cannot get close enough to violate your mental and emotional well-being. Rigid boundaries also don't make enough room for compromise during conflict resolution or adapting to unexpected work situations, like being asked by your manager to work an extra shift on the weekend.

Life happens, and you must be flexible enough to respond with appropriate actions whenever you are presented with challenges. Rigid boundaries keep you locked to your standards and expectations to the extent of not being a team player. On the other hand, you don't want to set boundaries that are too loose. Loose boundaries sound like a yes and a no. They are so blurred that people don't know how to respond to them.

Therefore, the ideal type of workplace boundaries is flexible enough to adapt to changing circumstances but clear enough to communicate well-defined limits. There are several types of boundaries that you can create at work. These include:

1. Physical Boundaries

The most basic types of boundaries limit access to your personal space and body. In most workplaces, rules about physical contact are written in company policy, but this doesn't mean that you can't assert them when necessary. Below are examples of how you can communicate physical boundaries:

- "I need to take a quick break to blow off some steam."
- "I won't be able to attend the meeting later on. I have a few assignments to complete by the end of the day."
- "Unfortunately, I'm not a hugger, but I would gladly shake your hand."
- "I can't focus while you are at my desk. Could we link up at lunchtime?"

Note that not every physical violation will be an assault of some sort. Any kind of physical contact that makes you feel uncomfortable or becomes a distraction needs a boundary.

2. Emotional and Intellectual Boundaries

It is important to protect your mental and emotional well-being at work by setting appropriate boundaries. This is another broad category, but essentially, these boundaries ensure that your ideas, beliefs, concerns, and feelings are respected. Below are a few examples of ways you can communicate emotional and intellectual boundaries:

- "This topic is making me uncomfortable. Can you excuse me?"
- "I need more time to think about that. Can I come back to you tomorrow?
- "We hold different views about this matter. Let's agree to disagree."
- "I didn't appreciate how you spoke to me yesterday. Calling me names was out of line."

To maintain strong emotional and intellectual boundaries, you will need to have a strong belief in yourself. You need to be confident enough to identify when you have been treated unfairly and invoke the inner warrior to speak up for you! Don't expect people to always understand where you are coming from because your emotional needs may be completely different from theirs. Sometimes, the best outcomes may be agreeing to disagree or limiting the number of interactions you have with a difficult colleague.

3. Workload Boundaries

It is healthy to set limits when it comes to how much workload you take on at any particular time, and which tasks you treat as priorities and non-urgent. Workload boundaries can be difficult to enforce because they turn down a coworker's request for support or assistance. But there are ways of being clear and assertive with your boundaries without offending the other person. Below are some ways of communicating workload boundaries:

- "I'm sorry to hear that you are short on staff, but my plate is quite full at the moment, and I won't be able to take on more work."

- "This deadline is too close for me. Can we push it back by two weeks?"
- "I would be happy to assist you with this project. My going rate is $150 per hour."
- "Yes, I will gladly accept this task. However, I can only start working on it after my short vacation. Are you comfortable with that?"

Realize that when coworkers ask for your help, it is an indication of your competence. It means that you are one of the few people they think of when they are looking for support. Therefore, if you are able to help, don't miss the opportunity to jump at the request. Being helpful, regardless of your position, can earn you a lot of respect.

4. Time Boundaries

There are plenty of distractions at work that can eat up your time. One major distraction is well-intentioned coworkers who interrupt you while you are working. If you have loose boundaries, you might allow coworkers to take up a lot of your time, including your personal time outside of the office. Below are a few examples of how you can communicate time boundaries:

- "I'm sorry, but I don't respond to emails after 4 pm."
- "Please do not disturb me before 10 am. The first few hours of the day are my most productive times."

- "I only have 30 minutes for this meeting. Can we please raise the most important issues first?"
- "Thank you for your email. I am out of the office and will respond to your message when I return."

Remember that your work style may be different from your coworkers and therefore it is important to explain how you structure your workday and the best and worst times to reach out to you. If you are working in a team, share your work calendar with the other teammates, so they can work around your schedule.

5. Communication Boundaries

Communication is a big part of getting work done. You need to define what are acceptable and unacceptable forms of communication at work, and how you would like others to reach out to you. Below are some examples of communication boundaries:

- "I don't typically text about work matters. Can we move this conversation to email or Slack?"
- "I would like to stay updated on the progress of this project. Please copy me in all of the email communication."
- "Please, may we keep the discussion strictly professional?"
- "My pronouns are she/her."
- "Please, may we respect the speaker and remain quiet during the presentation?"

It is okay to have moments where you are unreachable. If you are constantly available to talk or address problems, you may not have a lot of time to get through your tasks for the day. You can also set expectations about the kinds of information coworkers can share with you. For example, when someone requests a meeting to discuss their personal issues, you might suggest a better time to have the discussion with you or perhaps that they seek support from the employee support department if more appropriate.

Managing Up

Setting and enforcing healthy boundaries can feel daunting when the person you are dealing with is your manager. Ideally, you want to be comfortable approaching them with suggestions, concerns, or questions about your work. However, this kind of open and trusting relationship doesn't just happen; it must be nurtured over time.

Research has also shown that women of color have a harder time getting the attention of their higher-ups than white employees. It isn't so much that the manager isn't present in the office, but rather they are inaccessible, or are reluctant to give up their time and effort to help them thrive.

One of the strategies that women can use to get on their managers' radars and nurture a good relationship is to manage up. Managing up is about being proactive in shaping the kind of relationship you desire with your manager. Instead of waiting on them to make the first move, you set the tone and create reasonable expectations.

For example, when requesting a meeting with a busy manager, you might present it as a win-win situation to get them to be more receptive and engaged. You might even use empathy to learn more about what your manager's current goals are and find ways of aligning your work tasks with what they are focused on, too. This will give you something to bond over and hopefully lead to productive conversations.

Managing up is also about forming a partnership with your manager that is built on problem-solving together. However, in order for them to take you seriously, it is important to do your own homework and have relevant information to share. In other words, you should always position yourself as an asset to your manager so that they are willing to engage with you on a consistent basis. A few questions that can help you become an asset are:

- What information do you have that your manager doesn't know yet?
- What challenges is your team or department faced with that you are aware of?
- What information are you lacking? What is your strategy to get more clarity?

Keeping the lines of communication open is a mission you have to drive. One of the ways to do this is to understand your manager's leadership style, approach to work, and overall personality. The more you get to know them, the easier it is to filter the type of information you present to them. Below are a few questions to get to know your manager better:

- Is your manager relaxed or overbearing?
- Does your manager prefer micromanaging or collaboration?
- How does your manager make decisions? Are they more thoughtful or do they make quick decisions on the spot?

- What type of communicator is your manager?
- Does your manager prefer hard facts, or do they lean on their intuition?
- How is your manager's workday structured? How accessible are they during the day?

When you learn more about your manager and how they operate, you can adapt to their work, communication, and decision-making style and focus on topics that are most important to them. You will also have a greater appreciation for your manager's time, avoiding unnecessary meetings and conversations.

Another word of caution, more specifically for working women, is to avoid trying to please your manager. Indeed, it is important to have a good relationship with your manager, but it has to be based on merit, not pleasantries. For the relationship to be sustainable, there must be a quantifiable value that you bring to the table. When your focus is on being likable, you miss the opportunity of having real impact. Allow the quality of your work, and the level of detail and professionalism (as well as other traits) to persuade on your behalf. And if you are unable to gain recognition after all your hard work, it is okay to speak up for yourself, ask for feedback, and be more forthright about your strengths.

How to Deal With Difficult Coworkers

For many full-time workers, interacting with coworkers is something that cannot be avoided. Even with the shift to hybrid work schedules, there are many occasions where back-and-forth communication and collaboration are required. Having said this, working with a difficult coworker can affect your mental well-being and lead to reduced productivity. In extreme cases, it can cause you to fantasize about quitting your job, so you can get far away from them.

Besides working with difficult people, there will be times when you experience personality clashes with coworkers. Since your personality styles are not compatible, you may frequently enter conflicts or misunderstandings. For example, you might prefer a weekly project check-in and your team member might prefer a monthly check-in. Or you might prefer 15-minute meetings with a single agenda and your team member might prefer hour-long meetings with a long list of items to discuss.

Personality clashes are just as harmful to your mental health as working with difficult coworkers. Therefore, for the remainder of this section, we will treat these two types of work relationships as being one and the same thing. To deal with difficult coworkers, you need to have a level of detachment where you don't take everything that they say to heart. Recognize that their behavior has a lot to do with their personal struggles, perceptions, and attitudes. Even when their attacks are directed toward you, they are expressing their own hurt feelings.

Below are six types of difficult coworkers you are likely to meet in the workplace, and assertive strategies on how to respond to their behaviors:

1. The Gossiper

This individual feeds on office politics and rumors. They are usually informed about other people's work issues and take it upon themselves to spread the news with others. Most of the time, what they end up spreading is exaggerated information that can be damaging to a person's work reputation and can create unnecessary conflict. Some gossipers are aware of their harmful behavior and continue doing it for their entertainment. While other gossipers spread other people's information as a way to deflect from their own work situation.

How to respond: When a conversation turns into gossip, acknowledge that you have gone off-topic and return to the discussion you were having. You might say, "Jane, I will have to stop you because I think we have deviated from our original conversation. What were we speaking about again?" You can also interject by stating that you are not interested in other coworkers' issues and prefer to give them privacy in dealing with their personal or professional matters.

2. The Blamer

In work teams, you are likely to find an individual who is quick to point fingers at other people when they run into problems. This is almost an instinctive reaction for them that may stem from a fear of failure. For instance, by blaming someone else for the poor quality of work, they don't feel as guilty. A blamer may have also previously worked in a company where making mistakes came with serious consequences.

How to respond: Realize that the blamer often feels ashamed whenever things don't go their way. Besides being afraid to fail, they may also be a perfectionist. Reassure them that the issue can be resolved, and nobody is to be blamed. Mistakes are sometimes due to factors beyond human control; however, even if it was a human error, the situation can be seen as a learning opportunity, rather than a fault-finding mission. It is also important to redirect the blamer to the facts of a situation, because only facts can help you find solutions.

3. The Wildcard

A playing card that can represent any value, color, or suit is known as a wildcard. In the office, an individual who exhibits unpredictable behavior and tends to "go off" randomly is known as a wildcard. Their antics can be a cry for attention, but sometimes it may be due to a personality disorder like bipolar disorder or attention-deficit hyperactivity disorder (ADHD). When they are in a good mood, this person can entertain the entire team, but as soon as they are inconvenienced or are placed under stress, they may have trouble regulating their strong emotion. The impression that people often have of them is being unreliable and excessively driven by emotion.

How to respond: Communicate how their behavior affects you by using "I" statements, such as: "I feel nervous to give you constructive feedback because I am not sure how you will take it" or "When you walk into the office without greeting me on some days, I feel invalidated." During your engagements, check on your mental and emotional state. It's important to remain calm, even when they overreact, and continue speaking respectfully.

4. The Authoritarian

You will also come across people at work who are obsessed with being in control. This need for control has more to do with their personality than their job title. In some cases, it may be a symptom of obsessive-compulsive disorder (OCD). The authoritarian tends to hold a high work standard for themselves and others and will be nit-picky about how tasks should be carried out. If they are a manager, they will constantly look over your shoulder to see how you are coping with tasks and offer unsolicited advice.

How to respond: Figure out which battles are worth fighting with the authoritarian. When the task or situation is not that important to you, take a step back and allow them to lead. However, with that said, be clear about your work boundaries. When their actions violate your boundaries, like being micromanaged, pull them aside and set a boundary. Explain the negative effects of their behavior on your work performance and provide an alternative solution.

For example, you might say "Mike, I noticed you come over to my desk frequently during the day to check on my progress. Your check-ins cause me to lose focus on my work and it takes several minutes before I am back in the zone. I am starting to feel frustrated by this and would appreciate it if you would schedule a feedback meeting with me once a week instead."

5. The Victim

The victim is a team member who tends to complain a lot. They draw attention to their problems and look for sympathy from others. Sometimes, the victim might attempt to convince coworkers that a certain office issue is bigger than it is. This is done to gain support from fellow coworkers, so they can raise the issue with management. Similar to the blamer, the victim will point fingers when things go wrong and create a false narrative about what actually happened. For example, if they were mistakenly left out of an email, they might complain about being intentionally left out by their team members.

How to respond: Although the victim sounds like a five-year-old throwing a tantrum, it's important to be patient with them and respond respectfully. Due to their inferiority complex, they are fully convinced that others are constantly trying to find ways of putting them down or making their lives more difficult. Similar to the blamer, present the victim with undeniable facts about the situation and if they lean toward negative evidence, highlight the positive evidence.

Lastly, set clear boundaries to make sure you don't get pulled into their complaining. For example, you might say "I can imagine how stressful this situation is for you, but I need to get back to my work. Let's chat later!"

6. The Passive-Aggressive Type

Coworkers who conceal their true thoughts and feelings and pretend to be agreeable and pleasant display passive-aggressive tendencies. What makes them dangerous is that at any moment, they can retaliate or release their frustration through subtle acts of aggression, such as not meeting deadlines, "accidentally" losing documents, or turning coworkers against each other. It can be difficult to hold passive-aggressive people accountable for their behaviors because they do a good job of hiding their tracks or making their actions seem like innocent mistakes.

How to respond: Watch their body language carefully and see whether their words match their nonverbal gestures or facial expressions. For example, if the person says they are happy to go ahead with the plan, yet they ignore their team for the rest of the day, there is clearly more to how they are feeling than their words let on.

When approaching the passive-aggressive person, seek as much clarity as you can get! Explain what you are noticing from their body language and ask whether you are interpreting their behavior correctly. You can also let them know when their reactions look different from the natural response. For example, if they are seemingly happy after getting into a conflict with one of their coworkers, you can observe their behavior and mention that it is okay for them to feel upset after an argument.

These are just six types of difficult coworkers. I can guarantee you that there are plenty more types at your workplace. Dealing with each type requires a logical head and the ability to empathize with what they are experiencing. When you step into their shoes and see the situation from their perspective, you will be less offended by their actions and know the appropriate consequences or boundaries to enforce.

Become a Builder

The purpose of this entire chapter is to show you various ways to stand your ground at work. Think of it as the proactive approach to making the most of your current work circumstances. An important aspect of standing your ground is learning to be comfortable building relationships. In the previous section, we spoke about difficult work relationships, but not all relationships are challenging. In fact, there are some relationships you form in your career that open doors for future work opportunities, or learning experiences.

A study by McKinsey found that 50% of an organization's intellectual capital is a "relational asset" and 75% of a person's intellectual capital is their relationships (Leading Effectively Staff, 2020). This means that most of what you know about your industry, company, or position at work was learned by listening to somebody else. This could have been a lecturer in university, listening to a career podcast, reading industry books, or speaking to seasoned professionals who have walked the path you are on.

Having a solid professional network is not about how many people you know. It has more to do with the quality of your connections. Ideally, you want to build a diverse network of people with varied skills and experiences. You won't necessarily know everyone in your network on a personal level, and your connections won't all know each other too. However, there is still value that you can add to each other's professional lives.

Women are often reluctant to engage in networking due to underestimating their own capabilities. A study by Marjo-Riitta Diehl and colleagues found that women believe they will receive more value than they offer to their connections, hence not being proactive about building professional networks (Smith, 2022). The consequence of undermining themselves also means that women are more reliant on existing networks to present them with new work and learning opportunities.

However, there is only so much value a network will offer, until you need to expand your circle and get to know more people. There are four motivations that can make women excited about expanding their professional network. These include:

- The opportunity to grow your community, especially in industries where women are underrepresented.

- Joining networking organizations that connect women internationally, and provide business opportunities and support that you might not receive at your company.

- The potential to make genuine friendships, share personal and professional experiences, and work together to achieve common career goals.

- Having increased access to seasoned professionals, who can become your mentors over time, and provide a fresh perspective on your career.

Just like all sisterly friendships begin with two acquaintances, building your network will take a lot of time, patience, and intentionality. Below are a few networking tips that can help you start and nurture new professional relationships:

1. Confront Negative Ideas or Beliefs You Have About Networking

How does your perception of networking affect your willingness to get to know new people? Write down some old and existing negative beliefs you have about networking and reflect on how they have held you back from approaching new people, attending industry events, joining online groups, etc.

2. Audit Your Current Network Structure

Go onto your LinkedIn profile and look through your list of connections. Take a sample of at least 50 connections and assign them to different categories, such as "Previous Job," "Personal Friends," "Industry Peers," and "Micro-Community Peers." See which categories have the most and least people.

3. Make Authentic New Connections

Ask yourself if there are any people you would like to join the various categories. Write their names down in a different color. Then go back to LinkedIn and search for these people. If they are acquaintances, they may appear as 2nd-degree or 3rd-degree connections. Send them a connection request with a personal note explaining the intention of adding them to your network.

4. Do More Giving Than Receiving

Sincerity is key when connecting with new people. Avoid asking for favors or promoting products or services before you have built a foundation of trust. Remember, they may have heard about you, but they still need to learn who you are and what you are about. See the new connection as someone who might have a problem that you can solve. Be open to sharing your wealth of knowledge, industry advice, and strategies that have helped you get to where you are.

5. Find Ways to Increase Your Value

What sustains your network is consistently adding value to the lives of those you are connected to. This could be as simple as writing and posting a relatable article once a week. There must be something tangible that your network receives from you, on a regular basis, in order for the connection to remain fresh.

Note that you may need to learn new skills in order to provide more value to your connections. For example, if you are not a talented writer, sharpening your writing techniques can be one of your short-term goals, before setting up your blog.

6. Offer a Helping Hand

Be willing to empower those within your professional circle with skills and knowledge that you have accumulated over the years. It is a wonderful thing to gain a reputation as someone who is helpful because not only does it draw people toward you, but it also causes people to jump at the opportunity of helping you when you need support. Helping others won't always be about sharing information. Sometimes, the best way you can help another person is by recommending them to one of your other connections or spending an hour mentoring them every month.

7. Make Time to Meetup

Engagement is crucial to sustaining a strong network. Even when you cannot meet in-person, you can create opportunities to meet virtually. These meetups should be kept informal and conversational.

For example, you might ask for 10 minutes to introduce yourself to a new connection over Zoom. In larger group meetings, you may take the opportunity to ask questions related to your career goals. Note that these meetings are not supposed to be used for pitching unless you have made it clear to the other person beforehand. The purpose of these meetups is to make introductions, catch up with your network, and seek or offer support.

Here's what many professionals overlook about building strong networks: Forging meaningful relationships takes time. You shouldn't expect to get anything out of your network without offering value over an extended period of time. Warren Buffett once said, "It takes 20 years to build a reputation and five minutes to ruin it. If you think about that, you'll do things differently" (Snyder, 2017). Assuming that his statement is correct, what could you start doing today to strengthen and support your professional network today?

Practice Grace With Your Pace

Jennifer is a surgeon at a hospital in New Jersey. She spends a minimum of 50 hours per week at the hospital, working 12-hour shifts. A few years ago, her strenuous work schedule took a toll on her health and she experienced burnout. However, due to her passion for medicine and the supportive work environment, she decided to make a few lifestyle changes to reduce her vulnerability to stress.

Every morning, before hopping out of bed, she said a short prayer. This was followed by a 15-minute journaling session to write out her intentions for the day. She would reflect on these intentions while getting ready for work and on her commute to the hospital. The first few hours of her shift would go well. Her energy and social batteries were fully charged. However, halfway through her shift, the normal day-to-day demands of her job would start to feel more intense. Her mindset was still positive, but her tolerance levels were quickly diminishing.

After completing her rounds, she would head over to the break room. Set a timer for 10 minutes, and just sit quietly by herself. Sometimes, she would meditate and other times she would listen to how she is feeling at the moment and ask the question: What do I need right now? At times, her body would be dehydrated and drinking water would bring her energy levels back up. Other times, she would have personal matters weighing heavily on her mind, and writing down how she felt or making a phone call to a loved one made all the difference!

Jennifer noticed the positive changes in her attitude toward work. She was no longer returning home feeling worn out because self-care was a part of her daily work routine. Her infectious attitude also made a positive impact on her colleagues. She became the happy-go-lucky doctor that others would gravitate to whenever they needed a pick-me-up.

What is incredible about Jennifer's workplace breakthrough is that she didn't wait for her environment to change in order to make different decisions. It was as if she knew that reframing her thoughts and developing a positive mindset would transform her experience at work. By investing more into her physical, mental, and emotional well-being, she would go from being a self-sacrificing doctor to a self-preserving doctor, whose energy tank wouldn't run dry.

You don't need to wait for your work environment to improve before your experience at work improves. The power to effect change at your workplace begins with shifting your mindset and placing an emphasis on your well-being. It is about finding small ways to make progress while regulating your emotions and making sure that your needs are taken care of.

Don't allow the pursuit of perfection to be the enemy of your progress. You won't always perform at your optimum, coworkers won't always be easy to work with, and some work assignments will demand a lot more than you give. However, despite the pressures that you are up against, there is so much that you can do to make sure that you stay focused and motivated at work. Below are a few strategies that you can explore and personalize to improve your experience at work:

1. Define An Area You Would Like to Improve

The first step is directing your focus on one particular area of work you would like to improve. You might be tempted to think of multiple areas, but zone in on an area that depletes most of your energy or makes your experience at work feel overwhelming. If you are still unsure of what area to improve, reflect on the following questions:

- How do you currently spend your time at work?
- Who do you spend most of your time with?
- How do you feel about your workplace relationships?

- How satisfied are you with your current work schedule?
- How are you managing your workload or job responsibilities?
- Does your daily work routine work for you?
- How close are you to achieving your next career goal?
- What is the state of your physical, mental, and emotional health?

These questions will help you explore different aspects of your job and identify an area that could benefit from positive changes.

2. Get Off Autopilot

When you have accepted the status quo at work, you are no longer determined to make a difference in how you approach work. For example, if it is generally accepted at work that managers work grueling hours and don't have time for themselves, you might follow suit and become a manager who is overworked and cannot balance career demands with other aspects of your life. In other words, you go with the flow, but in the negative sense!

To make positive changes, you need to regain control of your mind and challenge norms that take a toll on your well-being. One way to do this is by dropping whatever limiting story you have told yourself about work, such as your work being a stressful environment, or that employees like you get looked over when promotions are given. These kinds of stories don't deserve your career advancement because they reinforce self-imposed limiting beliefs that keep you stagnant and complacent.

These beliefs also hold you back by keeping you on autopilot. For example, if you believe that despite how much work you put in, your efforts will never be noticed, you might stop working hard and instead do enough to cruise along without getting fired. In other words, your body is physically at work, but your mind has wandered off and you are unable to take different actions. For as long as you are running on autopilot, your work circumstances cannot improve because you don't have a sense of where you are, what needs to change, and what it will take to make the necessary changes.

3. Create Empowering Expectations

There is a quote by Henry Ford that I love, which says "Whether you think you can, or you think you can't, you're right" (Boomer, 2014). What he means is that you set the tone for your life. You cannot accomplish a goal that you are not fully convinced you can achieve. Your expectations are an indication of what you believe you can achieve. Setting low expectations for your work life does to some extent mean that you don't believe your circumstances can change.

The Pygmalion effect explains the power of expectations when it comes to relationships. According to this phenomenon, your expectations about other people change their behavior and performance. A study performed in the 1960s by psychologist Robert Rosenthal found that when teachers were told that certain students were expected to be high achievers in their classes, the students' marks actually improved (Van Edwards, 2020). How can the Pygmalion effect work for you? When you set empowering expectations about your work, your behavior and performance at work can improve to match those expectations.

You can become a better version of yourself at work by believing that you can be more and do more! Go back to the first strategy (finding an area of your work that can be improved) and set a few positive expectations. Make sure that these expectations give you a push to succeed, rather than pressure to be perfect.

4. Become a Continuous Learner

As mentioned in Step 2, one of the ways to get off autopilot is by increasing your appetite for learning. It is normal to get comfortable with work practices, your daily routine, and the stress-ridden life you are living, instead of searching for new information that can alleviate some of the burdens you are carrying.

Do you realize why people say, "Knowledge is power?" It is because the more information you learn, the greater your options for living the best possible life. For instance, someone who has learned the technique of meditation and read an article about journaling has more options when it comes to stress management than someone who has not discovered either strategy.

Being a continuous learner is also about recycling information that you already know and looking at circumstances from a new perspective. For example, if you have tried several coping strategies to deal with a difficult coworker and none of them have worked, you would assess each strategy, find the strengths and weaknesses, and consider how you can revise the strategy to work better in the future. You might find that adjusting a strategy, or combining positive elements of different strategies, can help you get through to the difficult coworker.

5. See Yourself as the Only Competition

The world of business is incredibly competitive. This is probably something you know and have accepted already. However, have you thought about what this means for your career?

Most professionals see the competitiveness of the corporate world as being a challenge to compete with their peers. Their thought process is: If I can work harder than X, I will be in a much better position to receive a raise. The danger with competing with others is that work becomes a sprint to the top, rather than a marathon that requires endurance. Most of the time, the pace at which the professional competes is too fast and unsustainable in the long run. This means that even if they manage to outperform their entire department, the professional cannot sustain the level of performance once they get to the top—this is often when burnout kicks in.

Going at your own pace means reframing who you see as competition. Instead of regarding your coworkers as competitors, you compete against former versions of yourself. In other words, you compare your current work performance to your performance six months ago and evaluate whether you have made progress or not. It will be clear which areas of your work need improvement, and whether you need to slow down or pick up the pace.

Gradually improving your work experience requires effort, and most of this effort will come from you. How badly do you want things to change at work? And what are you willing to do to bring about this change? You must *want* to have a better work life in order to make the mindset shift, carry out lifestyle changes, and do whatever else it takes to create a positive experience.

Remember, making progress is better than cruising on autopilot or seeking perfection. Once you get good at making one small change, you will have more confidence to commit to another small change!

STEP 5

End the Burnout Cycle—Evaluate Your New Path

> *I hope you remember that if you encounter an obstacle on the road, don't think of it as an obstacle at all... think of it as a challenge to find a new path on the road less traveled.*
>
> Hyeonseo Lee

Questions to Ask Yourself

Sometimes, the best way to gain clarity is not by seeking advice from a mentor or browsing on Google, but by asking yourself tough questions. Self-questioning sounds pretty straightforward on paper: You reflect on a certain area of life and ask yourself honest questions about it. However, asking yourself questions requires you to overcome the fear of the unknown.

There is a certain amount of courage needed to confront yourself about the truth of your situation. This is because you never know if how you are perceiving a situation is the most accurate representation of reality. For example, if you notice that your productivity has dropped at work, you might assume it has to do with how much you dislike your team members. But after doing some self-questioning, you may discover that your decreased productivity has more to do with increased responsibilities at home.

As uncomfortable as it may be to ask yourself questions, below are a few reasons why it is beneficial, especially on your journey to breaking the burnout cycle for good!

- **Gain clarity about the career path you are on.** Asking yourself questions can be a great way to assess if you are still on track to achieve your goals—or whether you are pursuing the *right* goals in the first place.

- **Get to know the real you.** Being able to describe who you are and what you want out of life and your career can reveal your strengths and weaknesses, and help you map out the best way to maximize your strengths in achieving your goals.

- **Understand your work environment.** How you experience your surroundings has a lot to do with your perception of what you see. Asking yourself questions about your work environment gives you a moment to step back and look objectively at your job and the relationships you have formed.

- **Gain clarity about your job role and responsibilities.** Self-questioning helps you look beyond your daily work routine and habits, and figure out what you are actually supposed to be doing (or what you are not obligated to do). This can later make setting work boundaries a lot easier because you are clear about your work duties.

Questioning your every move can cause you to detect burnout during its early stages and reverse the physiological and emotional effects immediately. At any given moment, you are able to work out if you are making the right career decisions and shift into problem-solving mode when you identify issues. The following sections will present a few questions that you can ask yourself related to your career development.

Questions About Your Job

If you would like to unlock your full potential at work, you need to honestly assess where you currently are, where you desire to be, and what you need to do to bridge the gap. You need to step back from your narrative about work and take on the role of an unbiased observer. Look at your job with these new pairs of eyes and determine what needs to change or what you need to continue doing more of. Below are questions to ask yourself about your job:

Question: What is your "WHY?"

Meaning: When we speak about a "WHY," we are referring to the driving force behind your decision to work and pursue your current career goals. The truth is, you didn't get to this stage of your career by accident and your goals must be rooted in something bigger than you. Discovering what that motivation was (or still is), can help you understand the importance of your job. Moreover, it can also help you evaluate whether the "WHY" is still relevant, or if it needs to be updated.

Question: What are you grateful for?

Meaning: Gratitude is the ability to notice and appreciate what you have. The reason why this is an important practice in your career is that it gives you a perspective of how far you have come so that you don't become complacent. Counting your career blessings can also be a reminder that you are capable of achieving whatever you set your mind to. During difficult moments at your job, you can encourage yourself by saying, "If I was able to overcome it before, I can overcome it again."

Question: Does your work align with your values?

Meaning: Your values are the foundational principles that make your life worth living. When what you do aligns with your core values, it carries a sense of meaning. Note that your job doesn't have to be your "dream job" for it to align with your values. For example, if you value security, then you might seek a full-time, permanent job, rather than a part-time or contractual job. If you are not yet clear about your values, take a moment to think about what matters most to you (you can focus strictly on your career). Thereafter, assess how many values your job aligns with. The result can be used as a measurement of how satisfied you are with your current job.

Question: Do you care more about how your job looks or feels?

Meaning: We are bombarded with images of success all over the internet. These images often portray a type of lifestyle that consists of flashy cars, a house in a gated neighborhood—and of course, an impressive job title. It is easy to get distracted by the image of being successful in your career (and the many doors that can be opened to you) and forget about the day-to-day demands of your job, maintaining a healthy work-life balance, and feeling like you are making a positive contribution to society.

Question: Do you see yourself within the same industry (or company) in the next 5–10 years?

Meaning: Even though it is hard to predict how your life will look in the next five to ten years, you intuitively know if you are in the right industry (or company), or not. For example, if you are unhappy with your current job and feel as though your true passion is somewhere else, then it is unlikely that you will remain in the same industry or company for much longer.

This question is supposed to encourage you to start planning your next year, or five years. If you don't see yourself staying in the company much longer, now is the best time to start planning your exit strategy. Alternatively, if you would like to grow within your industry or company, you can start mapping out your career growth strategy and the various milestones you will need to achieve to "bridge the gap."

Questions About Motivation

When you are motivated to work, you are more likely to experience high job satisfaction and increased productivity. Motivation can be seen as being extrinsic and intrinsic. Extrinsic motivation is driven by external achievements, symbols of success, or gaining recognition for what you do. In other words, you are motivated by the external rewards that your job offers. On the other hand, intrinsic motivation is driven by passion, positive feelings, and a sense of accomplishment. This type of motivation comes from within and isn't dependent on external factors.

Both extrinsic and intrinsic motivation can boost your morale and productivity at work. However, intrinsic motivation tends to be more sustainable in the long run. For example, when you are driven by an inner passion or purpose, your attitude toward work won't change, even when the tasks become monotonous. Or when your team experiences conflict and everybody seems divided, you are still able to focus and continue pushing yourself, despite not receiving the support you need.

The following questions are designed to help you explore how engaged and motivated you are with your current job. You can use the results from these questions to think of effective strategies to increase your intrinsic motivation.

Question: Are there any personal matters that are making it difficult to remain motivated at work?

Meaning: There are times when personal challenges with friends, family, finances, or your health can affect your enthusiasm and performance at work. If you answer "yes" to this question, you may need to adjust your work schedule or speak to your employee wellness manager to discuss ways of temporarily adjusting your work demands.

Question: Why do you love working for your company?

Meaning: It is important to reflect on why you love the company you work for. This goes back to showing gratitude for what you have. By answering this question, you can determine whether the pros of working at your company outweigh the cons, or vice versa. Focusing on the positive aspects of the company you work for can also reignite the passion you once had for what you do!

Question: Do you fully understand your role and responsibilities?

Meaning: One of the factors that contribute to low employee engagement is not being clear about what is expected from you. Perhaps you have not received the proper training for your job, or have been assigned specific duties by your manager. You might also have a poor relationship with your manager and don't feel confident to ask questions related to your job, or have clarity on how to complete some assignments.

Question: What inspires you to work hard in your role every day?

Meaning: Above and beyond loving your company, consider the personal reasons for being dedicated at work. What personal ambitions do you have that drive you to continuously seek to improve your performance at work? Note that this inspiration may have very little to do with your day job. For instance, you may be inspired to work hard because one day you hope to start your own business and will need as much expertise as possible to get it off the ground.

Question: Do you feel comfortable speaking your mind at work?

Meaning: Your job satisfaction is likely to increase when you feel valued at work. Feeling valued can be a result of many factors, however, one of them is having the opportunity to share your thoughts and feelings without any consequences to your reputation. In essence, you can disagree with your senior managers without the fear of being judged or being treated differently. This privilege allows you to voice concerns or offer suggestions whenever they arise, so you don't have to bottle feelings or turn a blind eye to situations that make you feel uncomfortable.

Question: Do you believe your company is helping you achieve your career goals?

Meaning: To feel happy at work, you want to rest assured that there are plenty of growth opportunities available to you. For example, you may want to move up the ranks of the company, receive regular salary raises, and be provided with skills training to advance your competencies. These are just some of the career goals that a company can assist you with. Determine what your company offers and whether their offer aligns with your career goals. It is also worth seeking clarity on how to qualify for certain career opportunities so that you can manage your expectations and begin bridging the gap immediately.

Questions About Productivity

Measuring productivity looks different depending on the profession you are in. There are some jobs, like manufacturing, where productivity can be measured in units produced, and other jobs, like customer service, where productivity is measured in specific metrics, such as the "Average Handle Time" (the average time an agent can keep the customer on the call).

Therefore, to assess your productivity at work, you may want to consider asking yourself questions about some of the following factors (depending on your job):

- Determine whether you are looking at qualitative outcomes or quantitative outcomes.
- Work out the percentage of goals completed in a specific period.
- Compare your performance in two periods, such as quarter one and quarter two.
- Evaluate your efficiency in completing a process, rather than the speed at achieving a result.
- Qualitatively assess the state of your physical, mental, and emotional well-being (you can also compare your well-being over two periods).

Below are a few questions that incorporate some of these factors. Note that you may need to customize the questions according to your work environment or job duties.

Question: How would you describe a typical day at work?

Meaning: You can measure your productivity by assessing how you structure your workday. A typical day means reflecting on the tasks you perform on a daily basis. A good sign of productivity is having a fixed work routine and following the same effective processes on a daily basis. If there is little structure to your day, then your productivity levels may fluctuate, which isn't a good sign.

Question: How do you manage distractions at work?

Meaning: There are plenty of distractions at home and at work vying for your attention. Some of these distractions can easily creep into your work time, like hearing a phone notification or having several tabs open on your laptop. If you are part of several work teams, the constant incoming messages from different work groups can also be distracting. It's important to have a plan on how you will manage distractions so you can enjoy uninterrupted work time. There are several productivity hacks that you can use, such as time blocking, muting notifications, or setting your status as "away" on instant messaging platforms like Slack.

Question: How do you manage your calendar?

Meaning: A calendar is a tool that can help you improve time management. Instead of filling it up with every small and big task, you can be more strategic about what tasks you accepted, the priority level of each task, and how much time you have allocated to complete them. Your calendar can even include five-minute rest breaks, spaced strategically throughout the day (i.e., Longer breaks when you need more time to recharge). Lastly, you can manage your calendar by screening every task and asking yourself whether it can be delegated to someone else, replaced with an email, or revisited later on in the week, month, or year.

Question: Are your physical and digital workspaces setting you up for success?

Meaning: Productivity begins in the mind. If your mind is chaotic, then it may be difficult to remain focused on your work tasks. However, a chaotic mind can also be triggered by a cluttered environment. Looking at your physical and digital workspaces can tell me a lot about your mental state. For example, when your office desk is full of clutter, it can be a reflection of the unrest in your mind. Making sure that your desk is clean and tidy, the chair is ergonomic, your email box has been emptied, and apps you don't use have been uninstalled are just some of the ways that you can increase your focus and set yourself up for success.

Question: How can you tell when the workday is over?

Meaning: We know that overworking is one of the leading causes of burnout. With the new hybrid work schedule and remote work opportunities, it is becoming crucial to determine when to stop working. It might be unrealistic to expect yourself to complete 100% of the day's tasks before you sign out. Remember, your company pays you to work for X number of hours per week and that can be divided into X number of hours per day.

Your office hours are there to protect the healthy balance between your personal and professional life, therefore frame your day around those parameters. You can also consider creating routines or rituals that you follow toward the end of the day, which signal to your body that you are approaching the time to close your laptop.

For example, you might dedicate 30 minutes in the mornings and afternoons to responding to emails. After responding to your emails, you might clean your office desk, followed by writing down tasks that need to be carried over the next day. In the last five minutes of your workday, you might decide to go through one of your music playlists and play a song while you pack your belongings, check your WhatsApp messages, and prepare to leave the office.

How to Choose a Coach, Therapist, or Other Helping Professional

Throughout this book, you have learned coping strategies to fight burnout on your own. However, depending on your needs and lifestyle, you can benefit from partnering with a coach,  therapist, or another mental health specialist who can hold your hand along the journey.

Remember, burnout occurs in a cycle, meaning even when you are able to successfully beat it this time around, it can reemerge after a few months, triggered by a new work-related situation. Following the five-step process will help you win the fight with burnout, but you may desire additional positive reinforcement from a coach or therapist. Other people may prefer to start working with a coach or therapist from the very beginning—the choice is all yours!

Please bear in mind that seeking help may not always make you feel comfortable, especially if you work in an environment where mental health and other work pressures are not spoken about openly. You may feel ashamed of being the only person on your team who cannot manage the work stress and just "suck it up." Nevertheless, your discomfort shouldn't stop you from taking a decision that can improve your physical, mental, and emotional well-being. You have so much to gain and very little to lose!

Now that you know that help is available, you will need to figure out what kind of support you need. Generally, there are coaches and therapists (or counselors) who are qualified to help you achieve your various career goals. Most of the time, coaches and therapists are seen as being one and the same thing, but their objectives and methods are completely different.

First, we should look at the definitions. A coach is an individual who provides expert guidance to their client to assist them in reaching their full potential. Even though they are not licensed healthcare professionals, they are knowledgeable in specific fields and can offer suggestions and pose reflective questions to the client, which they may not have considered. The client leads the conversation and does most of the talking, and the coach's job is to provide space for critical and abstract thinking.

On the other hand, a therapist, who might also be referred to as a counselor or psychologist, has gone to school and received training to offer psychological tools that help clients resolve emotional, behavioral, and relationship issues. The focus of therapy is to process and release past trauma, and combat self-destructive beliefs and habits that negatively affect the client's health, work, social life, or relationships.

A client can approach the coach and therapist with the same issue, but how the issue gets resolved will look different. Below are a few striking differences between the coach's and therapist's approaches to resolving personal issues:

- **The coach focuses on the present, while the therapist focuses on the past.** A coach will ask you questions about your current lifestyle, such as your diet, sleep, physical activity, etc. Their objective is to figure out how your current lifestyle choices are causing problems in your life. In contrast, a therapist is more interested in behavioral patterns that emerged from early childhood, which can explain how you think and respond to stressful situations.

- **The coach empowers you to take action, while the therapist helps you gain deeper self-awareness.** Coaching is action-oriented and often a coach will measure the client's progress by creating SMART goals and other performance metrics. A therapist empowers a client by teaching them about their subconscious thought patterns, which underpin their behaviors.

- **The therapist can support people with mental health problems, but the coach may not be qualified to do so.** Some of the common reasons clients seek counseling are to address mental health issues, such as PTSD, anxiety, chronic stress, and depression. Since coaches aren't required to be healthcare professionals, many of them may not have the training or qualifications to help with specific mental health conditions.

- **The therapist helps you cope with day-to-day stressors, while the coach helps you commit to positive life changes.** The role of a therapist is to teach you effective coping skills so that you can alleviate stress related to daily tasks. This is different from the coach's role, which is to help you adopt a new mindset and habits to achieve more out of your life.

Another type of professional that we haven't discussed yet is the mentor. A mentor is usually a friend, expert, or business connection that you have made, who has achieved amazing milestones within your industry. The role of a mentor is to impart skills and knowledge, as well as to make career recommendations and introduce you to the right people. The difference between a mentor and a coach or therapist is that the former is strictly focused on your career development and may not be able to advise you on personal issues.

Furthermore, since they tend to not charge you for their time, you have limited access to them (their availability depends on their work schedule). They may also expect you to have a list of questions prepared for them or completed assignments to present during your meeting. In other words, they want to see evidence that you value their time and expertise by making progress on your own and arriving to meetings with an outlined agenda of things to discuss.

Coaching, therapy, and mentorship are all useful at various stages of your career. Depending on which stage of the burnout cycle you are in, you might opt for a specific kind of helper. You can use this handy checklist below to guide you in choosing the right professional according to your needs:

Speak to a coach when you need:

- Assistance with setting and achieving career goals.
- Support on creating and pitching a business plan.
- Techniques to improve your communication skills.
- Strategies to improve your work-life balance.
- Advice on making a career transition/starting a new business.

Speak to a therapist when you need:

- Support to recover from past trauma.
- Support to manage anxiety and depression, which affects your performance at work.
- Skills on how to handle difficult coworkers and set effective boundaries.
- Skills on how to cope with stressful seasons at work.
- Support with overcoming low self-esteem and

imposter syndrome.

Speak to a mentor when you need:

- Advice on how to map out the next five years of your career.
- Strategies to overcome workplace challenges, such as being overworked, underpaid, or discriminated against.
- Techniques on how to grow your professional network, and the right people to approach.
- An outsider to hold you accountable to achieve your career ambitions.
- Support on how to manage symptoms of burnout.

If you ask any successful professional how they got to the top, they will mention the support of their parents, mentors, and coaches. This goes to show that nobody arrives at the top by climbing alone. We all need to find our people, who can cover our weaknesses and give us a boost of confidence when we need it most.

BONUS

Managing a Team in Burnout

Sometimes the bravest and most important thing you can do is just show up.

Brené Brown

Signs of Burnout in Employees

We have gone through the five steps to ARISE out of the burnout cycle. However, the five steps were geared toward your physical, mental, and emotional recovery. This bonus chapter is dedicated to managers, team leaders, or entrepreneurs who are managing a team that is experiencing burnout. Instead of taking them through the five-step ARISE process, it is important to examine your work practices and culture, which could be triggers that cause burnout.

The first step is to recognize the signs of employee burnout. The earlier you catch these signs, the quicker you can reverse the consequences of burnout and restore balance in your team. Here are a few common signs that you can look out for:

1. Employee Engagement Has Declined

When your employees no longer take pride in their work, miss deadlines, or refuse to participate in work meetings, it is a sign of low engagement. Don't get me wrong. Nobody is expected to be in good spirits all of the time, but a gradual decline in enthusiasm about work is not a good sign.

2. Silly, Avoidable Mistakes Are Being Made

You are aware of your team's caliber of performance. You know when they have worked hard on a project and when it was a rushed job. When you notice a lot of unnecessary mistakes being made, like failing to double-check figures, cutting corners, or using old information instead of recent data, take it as a sign that they may be overwhelmed and distracted.

3. Your Team Members Are Absent Frequently

High absenteeism is not a good indicator of happy employees. Research shows that employees who are experiencing burnout are 63%

more likely to request sick days. Besides falling sick, other reasons for taking time off work could be feeling exhausted or stressed about the thought of going to work.

4. Your Team Members Are Moody

If you spend a lot of time with your team, you might notice changes in their attitudes. For instance, someone who is normally cracking jokes has become increasingly cynical about their work tasks, or employees who normally get along with each other have been getting into conflicts. Other behavioral changes that you can look out for are emotional detachment, self-doubt, loss of motivation, and a sense of helplessness.

5. Changes In Social Habits

Another sign of employee burnout is changes in social habits. Some team members may isolate themselves from others and only speak when it is necessary. Other team members may become chattier as a way to avoid sitting at their desks and completing their stressful work tasks. You may also see divisions within the team caused by poor communication and microaggression. Some employees may also take advantage of relaxed work rules, like coming into work late because they are not expected to clock in at a certain time.

Burnout-Busting Strategies to Implement at Work

Not every stress-related incident at work is a sign of burnout. Sometimes, employees react unfavorably due to personality clashes with other team members, personal issues at home, or poor self-control. Burnout symptoms often continue for an extended period of time and affect different areas of work, such as productivity, relationships, and motivation.

As a manager or leader, there are effective strategies you can implement with your team whenever you suspect they might be experiencing burnout. These strategies include:

- **Show random acts of appreciation.** Surprise your employees with rewards for their continued good work. It doesn't have to be a big reward, but something meaningful that shows how much you value their efforts. Employees that feel valued are able to remain engaged and withstand difficult times on the job.

- **Respect off-duty boundaries.** When your employees are not at work, avoid reaching out to them via email, text, or phone call. Be considerate of their need for rest and to spend quality time with loved ones. The same applies when one of your team members is on vacation—resist the urge to make contact with them!

- **Be mindful of how much you communicate.** Excessive communication means reaching out too much. This could be sending a chain of text messages, receiving the same message through different channels, or making every meeting mandatory (even those that are not relevant to the completion of work tasks). Cut down on the frequency of communication and ensure that your messages are worthwhile and reach the relevant people.

- **Provide your team with a platform to speak.** Whenever employees feel like their voice doesn't matter, they can feel powerless over their work situation. Create a platform or ritual that allows employees to voice their concerns, give feedback, and offer suggestions. Before making big decisions that affect the team, take a moment to inform your team and ask them to share their opinions.

- **Encourage work habits that relieve stress.** Create new cultural practices in your team that allow employees to relieve stress during work hours. For example, you can encourage listening to music through headphones while working, creating a quiet corner where people go to read or meditate, or being flexible about what kind of clothing employees wear to work. You can also make mental health a priority by encouraging several rest breaks during the day, working outside, or offering discounted counseling services.

- **Lead by example.** As a manager or leader, you set the pace and attitude at work. One of the ways to encourage self-care is to see yourself as a role model and adopt values and behaviors that show a harmonious work-life balance. When your team notices how you manage stress, the priority you place on rest, and other productive habits, they will be inspired to emulate you and make adjustments to their work practices too!

Your early intervention can save your team from going through the cycle of burnout. Plus, when employees see your willingness to combat a toxic work environment, they will feel seen, heard, and supported. Don't be shy to speak about the realities of burnout with your team and ask for suggestions on policy updates or alternative work practices. This is just another way to make them feel included in decision-making and increase their engagement at work.

Watch Your Words

Malaika came out fresh from university and started out at a junior position at her company. She was understandably overwhelmed by the demands of her job, even though she didn't dare tell anyone about it. Her strategy was to go with the flow and pretend she knew what was expected of her. However, after a few weeks, her manager called a meeting and sat down with her to give a feedback session.

During the meeting, the manager told her how disappointed they were by her performance and implied that if she didn't make serious changes, she could end up being fired. Malaika knew that the manager was fair to call her out on her low performance. However, their words worsened her anxious feelings and made her feel even more afraid and stressed out. Now, even if she wanted to ask for help, she was scared that it would jeopardize her reputation.

Managers and leaders aren't always mindful of their choice of words. Expressing disapproval may seem warranted, but what about the impact that those words have on the employee's morale? For example, take the phrase, "I'm busy." How many managers and leaders weigh the cost of uttering that phrase? While it is true that you are busy, the phrase can come across as shutting down an employee's request for help or invalidating their feelings. They may walk away thinking, "Whatever I had to say doesn't matter to my boss."

Or how about the phrase, "That's not my fault." When an employee hears this from their manager, they can feel helpless. After all, if the manager won't take responsibility or show interest in resolving a work issue, who else will? Once again, it may be true that the issue has nothing to do with the manager; however, since they are in a leadership role, it is their job to provide guidance and support to employees, even if it means pointing them to someone who might be more suitable to help.

Another hurtful phrase that employees hear a lot is, "This is how we have always done things." A manager might say this after listening to an employee complain about a tedious work process. Instead of stepping into the other's shoes and seeing the situation from their perspective, the manager dismisses the proposal and clings to tradition. What the employee hears is, "My satisfaction at work is not considered." It could also make the employee reluctant to bring forward innovative solutions in the future.

It is important to be considerate of where each team member is on their career path and the kind of support they need. Being overly critical of the new intern's job performance may not be the best way to support them and make them feel appreciated at work. Perhaps what they need is more positive affirmations of what they are doing well. This might give them the boost of confidence that they are lacking.

It is also worth considering how your words can be interpreted. Think about the message you want to convey and how you desire the employee to feel once you have communicated it. Doing this will help you choose words that match your positive intention.

For example, if you want to let an employee know that arriving late to work is unacceptable, but you want them to leave feeling encouraged to take action, you might say, "Dina, I noticed that you have a habit of arriving late to work. I feel offended when you do this because it comes across like you don't care about the rules. You are the energizer on our team, and we would like to start our morning with your positive spirit. Can you work on arriving on time?"

The only time when you don't have to watch your words is when you are giving praise! Employee recognition is a great way to boost your team's morale and make them feel like a valuable member of the company. Find opportunities to give genuine recognition for good work—or even progress! Be sure to mention what the good behavior was, and how it positively impacted you (or the team). Here are 10 ways to say thank you to your awesome team members:

- It is because of your dedication that we have surpassed our target. Thank you!

- You inspire me with your positive attitude. Keep it up!
- Thank you for all the effort you have been putting in lately. This team wouldn't be the same without you.
- Your attention to detail blows my mind every time. You are truly incredible!
- I am so proud of your growth on this team. You are flourishing right before my eyes.
- You exceeded my expectations with this assignment. Kudos to you!
- I know I have been busy lately, but I just wanted to stop by and say how much I value your contribution to the team. Thank you for being here.
- I love to hear your ideas. Keep them coming!
- I am such a lucky manager to have you as part of my team. I am always here if you need anything.
- Your willingness to produce high-quality work consistently is admirable. You inspire me to keep going. Thank you!

Whether you realize it or not, your team wants to make you proud. They seek your validation as assurance that they are making progress and adding value to the company. Never miss an opportunity, regardless of how big or small, to let your team know that you are watching and are incredibly proud of them.

Conclusion

If I had to embrace a definition of success, it would be that success is making the best choices we can.

Sheryl Sandberg

Women continue to suffer alarming rates of burnout in the workplace, but you won't hear much about it. Why? Because working in largely male-dominated corporate environments causes many women to seek to prove that they deserve to be there.

The great lengths that you go through seeking validation and recognition cause you to undermine your performance, become self-critical, and take on more responsibilities than you can bear.

In this modern world, being a working woman is an incredible achievement. However, that is not the sum total of everything you are as a woman. You can also be someone's daughter, sister, friend, mother, spouse, or mentor. Each of these roles requires an investment of time, meaning that in order to feel whole and enjoy your life, your attention cannot be solely focused on work.

As defined earlier in the book, burnout is workplace stress that is characterized by exhaustion, cynicism, and reduced work efficacy. When exploring the causes of burnout, we found that it wasn't just the work relationship that contributed to the chronic feelings of tiredness and dissatisfaction. The main culprit was the lack of a harmonious work-life balance, which meant that too much time, energy, and attention was being invested in a single area of your life—leaving your health, hobbies, social life, and relationships on the back burner.

The two other "B" words that can break the cycle of burnout in your life are balance and boundaries. Nothing that is done to the extreme is ever good for you, even if it starts off feeling satisfying. Your sense of peace in life can be found when you move away from the extremes and learn how to divide your time between areas of your life that are important to your overall well-being. But to maintain balance you will need to enforce solid boundaries that make sure that you don't neglect one area of your life at the expense of another.

In the long run, preventing burnout is about confronting the triggers and lifestyle habits, and clearly defining what success means to you based on your identified core values. Remember that success can look different at various stages of your life and career, so making sure to check in with yourself at each stage is important.

Conclusion

The aim of this book was to teach you how to confront and overcome burnout by prioritizing balance and boundaries. You were taken through five steps to break the burnout cycle and ARISE from the tired and miserable routines that brought little satisfaction and much pain! The five steps can be summarized as follows:

STEP 1: Act Now—Build Your Short-Term Recovery Plan

STEP 2: Reset The Dial In Your Life—Relax! The Building Won't Collapse Without You

STEP 3: Invoke Your Inner Warrior—Reignite Your Passion For Your Career Goals

STEP 4: Stand Your Ground—No Backsies!

STEP 5: End The Burnout Cycle—Evaluate Your New Path

These steps include both a short and long-term strategy to address burnout, and plenty of strategies that you can customize to suit your personal and professional needs. To get the most out of these steps, you need to be willing to put in the work by asking yourself tough questions, being open to venture out of your comfort zone, and adjusting your attitude toward your life.

When your attitude and approach to each area of your life changes, you will find that you have enough time and motivation to live out your wildest dreams!

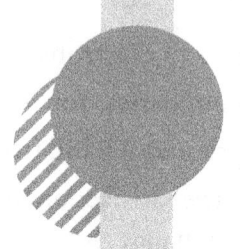

If you enjoyed this book, and found its contents useful, please leave us a review on Amazon

US:

http://www.amazon.com/review/create-review?&asin= B0BLT5JHM3

UK:

http://www.amazon.co.uk/review/create-review?&asin= B0BLT5JHM3

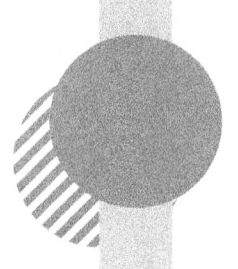

About The Author

Kai-Nneka Townsend is an author and Programme Manager, who lives in the UK. Since the age of 17 she has lived in various countries across the globe for work and study. Having gone through burnout herself throughout her earlier career, she is passionate about helping women recognize the signs of burnout early and get the help they need to take action and move from a place of surviving, to thriving in their career journey.

She is also a children's book author and loves creating work that helps prepare the next generation of women to feel empowered and valued, not just for what they can do for this world, but who they are as a person.

To get in touch about:

- Coaching on how to break your burnout cycle
- Speaking engagements
- Workshops on strategies for women to achieve success without burnout, or

- Bulk copies of this book

Please connect with us at:

Email: connect@kainnekatownsend.com

Or visit our website for more information

www.kainnekatownsend.com

References

Abdilova, L. (2020, June 19). *The difference between a mentor, career coach, and therapist.* The Muse. https://www.themuse.com/advice/mentors-career-coaches-and-therapists-which-ones-best-to-get-you-out-of-your-rut

Angshuman. (2019, April 4). *50 Best words of appreciation for employees you can't ignore.* Vantage Circle HR Blog. https://blog.vantagecircle.com/words-of-appreciation-for-employees/

Become Team. (2021, November 17). *Women's guide to self-advocacy and salary negotiation at work.* LearnHowToBecome.org. https://www.learnhowtobecome.org/career-resource-center/womens-guide-to-self-advocacy/

Boomer, J. (2014, July 15). *Whether you think you can, or think you can't … you're right.* CPA Practice Advisor. https://www.cpapracticeadvisor.com/2014/07/15/whether-you-think-you-can-or-think-you-cant-youre-right/15980/

The Calmer Team. (2020, August 20). *What are the 5 stages of burnout?* Calmer. https://www.thisiscalmer.com/blog/5-stages-of-burnout

Castillo, D. (n.d.). *How women can build a professional network from home.* Live Career. https://www.livecareer.com/resources/women-at-work/career-advancement/professional-network-from-home

Charatan, D. (2017, September 22). *How women can define success on their own terms.* Medium. https://medium.com/@debrahcharatan/how-women-can-define-success-on-their-own-terms-8eee3d76459f

Complete Payroll. (n.d.). *Six essential tips to help burned out employees.* Blog.completepayroll.com. https://blog.completepayroll.com/six-essential-tips-to-help-burned-out-employees

Daly, A. (2020, March 3). *The real reason exercise makes you happy, according to research on the brain.* Mindbodygreen. https://www.mindbodygreen.com/0-10798/6-reasons-why-exercise-makes-you-happy.html

Daskal, L. (2020, June 19). *7 Things you should start doing today to be successful tomorrow.* The Muse. https://www.themuse.com/advice/7-things-you-should-start-doing-today-to-be-successful-tomorrow

Eatough, E. (2021a, June 10). *How to create a life plan (a life planning template).* Betterup.com. https://www.betterup.com/blog/life-planning

Eatough, E. (2021b, July 30). *Setting boundaries in relationships: A how-to.* Www.betterup.com. https://www.betterup.com/blog/setting-boundaries?hsLang=en

Eatough, E. (2021c, October 25). *How to recover from burnout and love your life again.* Www.betterup.com. https://www.betterup.com/blog/how-to-recover-from-burnout

Ellevate. (n.d.). *Passion in your career quotes*. Www.ellevatenetwork.com. https://www.ellevatenetwork.com/articles/6173-passion-in-your-career-quotes

Elsesser, K. (2022, March 14). *Women are suffering from an "exhaustion gap" according to new study*. Forbes. https://www.forbes.com/sites/kimelsesser/2022/03/14/women-are-suffering-from-an-exhaustion-gap-according-to-new-study/?sh=69fcb71037b3

Freedman, M. (2022, August 5). *10 Tips for a successful job exit*. Business News Daily. https://www.businessnewsdaily.com/6116-how-to-quit-your-job-without-burning-bridges.html

Geannette, M. (2021, September 6). *15 Tips to inspire change in your life*. Clever Girl Finance. https://www.clevergirlfinance.com/blog/change-in-your-life/

Gerencer, T. (2019, October 8). *Burnout: Prevention, treatment, and advice for employees and employers*. Zety. https://zety.com/blog/burnout?utm_source=google&utm_medium=sem&utm_campaign=6540106315&utm_term=%2Bburnout&network=g&device=c&adposition=&adgroupid=85084943440&placement=&gclid=CjwKCAjw-8qVBhANEiwAfjXLrhPo1_7E5XK916p-ttp_4LBnZvxTrvRXYR-x8wcm7lDj1lkH9sFXohoCJ-QQAvD_BwE

Goldberg, M. (2021, June 28). *Feeling burned out? These expert-approved strategies will help you recover*. Oprah Daily. https://www.oprahdaily.com/life/a36801181/how-to-recover-from-burnout/

Good Reads. (n.d.-a). *Hyeonseo Lee quote*. Www.goodreads.com. https://www.goodreads.com/author/show/7785294.Hyeonseo_Lee

Good Reads. (n.d.-b). *Katherine May quote*. Www.goodreads.com. https://www.goodreads.com/author/show/611020.Katherine_May

Good Reads. (n.d.-c). *Richelle E. Goodrich quote*. Www.goodreads.com. https://www.goodreads.com/author/show/5082833.Richelle_E_Goodrich

Good Reads. (n.d.-d). *Sheryl Sandberg quote*. Www.goodreads.com. https://www.goodreads.com/author/show/5333595.Sheryl_Sandberg

Good Reads. (n.d.-e). *Take action quotes (135 quotes)*. Www.goodreads.com. https://www.goodreads.com/quotes/tag/take-action

Good Reads. (n.d.-f). *Vanessa Autrey quote*. Www.goodreads.com. https://www.goodreads.com/author/show/21958457.Vanessa_Autrey

Ha, K. (2021, June 7). *My failed legal career is the perfect example of sunk costs*. The Post-Grad Survival Guide. https://medium.com/the-post-grad-survival-guide/my-failed-legal-career-is-the-perfect-example-of-sunk-costs-e710bd04b102

Harris, H. (2022, January 19). *5 Major signs of employee burnout and how to address them*. Nivati. https://nivati.com/blog/5-major-signs-of-employee-burnout-and-how-to-address-them/

Howden, D. (2016, October 25). *The dishonest myth of work-life balance*. Recruiting Resources: How to Recruit and Hire Better. https://resources.workable.com/stories-and-insights/work-life-balance-myth

Indeed Editorial Team. (2021, February 23). *12 Motivation questions to ask employees*. Indeed Career Guide. https://www.indeed.com/career-advice/career-development/motivation-questions-for-employees

Kehayas Holden, C. (n.d.). *5 Things your job shouldn't be (and what it should be)*. Career Contessa. https://www.careercontessa.com/advice/what-is-a-career/

Kelly, D. C. (n.d.). *48 Quotes about hard work that'll help you reach your goals*. Blog.hubspot.com. https://blog.hubspot.com/sales/hard-work-quotes

Kumar, A. (2020, October 4). *Why is it important to question yourself often*. Age of Awareness. https://medium.com/age-of-awareness/why-is-it-important-to-question-yourself-often-7e39fd5f62fa

Le Cunff, A.-L. (2021, March 16). *Mindful productivity audit: 10 Questions to improve your well-being at work*. Ness Labs. https://nesslabs.com/mindful-productivity-audit

Leading Effectively Staff. (2020, November 11). *4 Ways women can build a network that advances their career*. Center for Creative Leadership. https://www.ccl.org/articles/leading-effectively-articles/women-is-your-network-working-for-you/

Leisenring, M. (2020, March 31). *Equal pay day is March 31 – the earliest since it began in 1996*. The United States Census Bureau. https://www.census.gov/library/stories/2020/03/equal-pay-day-is-march-31-earliest-since-1996.html

Leiter, M. P., & Maslach, C. (2016). *Latent burnout profiles: A new approach to understanding the burnout experience.* Burnout Research, 3(4), 89–100. https://doi.org/10.1016/j.burn.2016.09.001

Loflin, J. (2022, September 1). *10 Questions to measure your personal productivity.* Www.linkedin.com. https://www.linkedin.com/pulse/10-questions-measure-your-personal-productivity-jones-loflin/?trk=public_post

Luenendonk, M. (2019, September 25). *15 Life-changing questions to ask yourself today.* Cleverism.com. https://www.cleverism.com/15-life-changing-questions-to-ask-yourself-today/

May, R. W., Terman, J. M., Foster, G., Seibert, G. S., & Fincham, F. D. (2020). *Burnout stigma inventory: Initial development and validation in industry and academia.* Frontiers in Psychology, 11. https://doi.org/10.3389/fpsyg.2020.00391

Merlo, G., & Rippe, J. (2020). *Physician burnout: A lifestyle medicine perspective.* American Journal of Lifestyle Medicine, 155982762098042. https://doi.org/10.1177/1559827620980420

Michaels, G. (2021, June 15). *5 Types of boundaries to start setting with your team.* Blog.trello.com. https://blog.trello.com/boundaries-to-start-setting-with-your-team

Millard, E. (2021, September 29). *Struggling with mental burnout? Aerobic exercise—like running—may help your brain recover.* Runner's World. https://www.runnersworld.com/news/a37727325/running-may-help-you-recover-from-mental-burnout-study/

Nedio, I. (2020, May 4). *How networking supports women's career development.* Accedo. https://www.accedo.tv/how-networking-supports-womens-career-development/

Nichols, K. (2020, April 15). *Do I need a counselor or a coach?* Happiful Magazine. https://happiful.com/do-i-need-a-counsellor-or-a-coach/

Nieuwhof, C. (2019, February 15). *11 Signs you're more than just tired…you're burning out.* CareyNieuwhof.com. https://careynieuwhof.com/11-signs-youre-more-than-just-tired-youre-burning-out/

Panel®, E. (2021, October 18). *Council post: 15 Empowering ways to advocate for yourself at work.* Forbes. https://www.forbes.com/sites/forbeshumanresourcescouncil/2021/10/18/15-empowering-ways-to-advocate-for-yourself-at-work/?sh=209de4f77b03

Pearl, R. (2022, April 26). *Physician burnout is increasing, gender inequality is making it worse.* Forbes. https://www.forbes.com/sites/robertpearl/2022/04/26/physician-burnout-is-increasing-gender-inequality-is-making-it-worse/?sh=83df5986eab4

Perry, E. (2022, February 10). *The right way to ask for time off— How to do it successfully.* Www.betterup.com. https://www.betterup.com/blog/how-to-ask-for-time-off

Porges, M. (2021, February 3). *Women entering the workforce— Here's how to get what you want.* Harvard Business Review. https://hbr.org/2021/02/women-entering-the-workforce-heres-how-to-get-what-you-want

Rebel Blends. (2020, June 11). *Self care checklist-An idea guide for mind, body and soul.* Rebel Blends. https://rebelblends.co/blogs/tips/self-care-checklist-an-idea-guide-for-mind-body-and-soul

Reichard, G. (2021, September 3). *How to reset your life.* WikiHow. https://www.wikihow.com/Reset-Your-Life

Robbins, T. (2016). *Life coach vs. Therapist, learn the difference.* Tonyrobbins.com. https://www.tonyrobbins.com/coaching/life-coach-vs-therapist/

Sandrini, M. (2019, October 30). *5 Tough lessons from quitting my full-time job to start a business.* Ladders. https://www.theladders.com/career-advice/5-tough-lessons-from-quitting-my-full-time-job-to-start-a-business

Schoppe-Sullivan, S. (2017, February 3). *Dads are more involved in parenting, yes, but moms still put in more work.* The Conversation. https://theconversation.com/dads-are-more-involved-in-parenting-yes-but-moms-still-put-in-more-work-72026

Singh, R., Volner, K., & Marlowe, D. (2022). *Provider burnout.* PubMed; StatPearls Publishing. https://www.ncbi.nlm.nih.gov/books/NBK538330/#:~:text=National%20studies%20suggest%20that%20over

Smith, J. (2022, April 6). *Women don't network as much because they undervalue themselves.* Workplace Insight. https://workplaceinsight.net/women-dont-network-as-much-because-they-undervalue-themselves/

Snyder, B. (2017, May 1). *7 Insights from legendary investor Warren Buffett.* CNBC. https://www.cnbc.com/2017/05/01/7-insights-from-legendary-investor-warren-buffett.html#:~:text=2.

Stybel, L. (2022, March 4). *Why work-life balance is a myth.* Www.psychologytoday.com. https://www.psychologytoday.com/gb/blog/platform-success/202203/why-work-life-balance-is-myth

Tucker, A. (2019, May 29). *25 Motivational quotes that'll get you through a rough day at work.* Woman's Day. https://www.womansday.com/life/work-money/g27460287/motivational-quotes-for-work/?slide=17

Universal Class. (2009). *10 Difficult workplace personalities and how to deal with them.* UniversalClass.com. https://www.universalclass.com/articles/business/difficult-workplace-personalities-and-how-to-deal-with-them.htm

Van Edwards, V. (2020, May 13). *10 Life-changing steps to become the best version of yourself.* Science of People. https://www.scienceofpeople.com/best-version-of-yourself/

WBT Systems. (n.d.). *Aging members will stick around (and keep learning) longer than you think.* Www.wbtsystems.com. https://www.wbtsystems.com/learning-hub/blogs/aging-members-working-learning-longer

Wooll, M. (2021, August 16). *A guide to changing your career at any stage.* Www.betterup.com. https://www.betterup.com/blog/guide-to-changing-career

World Health Organization. (2019, May 28). *Burn-out an "occupational phenomenon": International classification of diseases*. Www.who.int. https://www.who.int/news/item/28-05-2019-burn-out-an-occupational-phenomenon-international-classification-of-diseases

Wynter, K. (2018, October 6). *Secret strategies powerful women use to overcome perfectionism and build courage*. Your Power Unleashed. https://www.yourpowerunleashed.org/blog/yourpowerunleashedcom/secret-strategies-powerful-women-use-to-overcome-perfectionism-and-build-courage

Yang, S. (2020, September 19). *The daily mental health habit that makes a big difference*. TheThirty. https://thethirty.whowhatwear.com/how-to-check-in-with-yourself/slide9

Image References

Fauntleroy, C. (2020). *Photo of woman resting on the couch [Online Image]*. In Pexels. https://www.pexels.com/photo/photo-of-woman-resting-on-the-couch-4270365/

Fauntleroy, C. (2021). *A woman standing in front of her colleagues [Online Image]*. In Pexels. https://www.pexels.com/photo/a-woman-standing-in-front-of-her-colleagues-8154798/

Fauxels. (2019). *Colleagues shaking each other's hands [Online Image]*. In Pexels. https://www.pexels.com/photo/colleagues-shaking-each-other-s-hands-3184291/

Fortunato, W. (2021). *Ethnic woman kissing baby near netbook and coffee cup [Online Image]*. In Pexels. https://www.pexels.com/photo/ethnic-woman-kissing-baby-near-netbook-and-coffee-cup-6392997/

Gambardella, J. (2020). *A woman in brown shirt typing on her laptop while sitting beside her kids [Online Image]*. In Pexels. https://www.pexels.com/photo/a-woman-in-brown-shirt-typing-on-her-laptop-while-sitting-beside-her-kids-6212715/

Grabowska, K. (2021). *Woman writing with a pen [Online Image]*. In Pexels. https://www.pexels.com/photo/woman-writing-with-a-pen-7320613/

Grabowska, K. (2022). *Woman in front of a laptop [Online Image]*. In Pexels. https://www.pexels.com/photo/woman-in-front-of-a-laptop-8547196/

Krukov, Y. (2021a). *A group of people discussing [Online Image]*. In Pexels. https://www.pexels.com/photo/a-group-of-people-discussing-7640781/

Krukov, Y. (2021b). *A tired woman massaging her head [Online Image]*. In Pexels. https://www.pexels.com/photo/a-tired-woman-massaging-her-head-8867180/

Magnet.me. (2020, August 24). *Woman in blue long sleeve shirt using silver Macbook*. Unsplash.com. https://unsplash.com/photos/315vPGsAFUk

Milton, G. (2021). *Cheerful diverse women having conversation during interview [Online Image]*. In Pexels. https://www.pexels.com/photo/cheerful-diverse-women-having-conversation-during-interview-6953855/

Morillo, C. (2018). *Person using Macbook Air [Online Image]*. In Pexels. https://www.pexels.com/photo/person-using-macbook-air-1181555/

Nilov, M. (2021). *Person people woman relaxation [Online Image]*. In Pexels. https://www.pexels.com/photo/person-people-woman-relaxation-7530023/

RF Studio. (2020). *Women at the meeting [Online Image]*. In Pexels. https://www.pexels.com/photo/women-at-the-meeting-3810795/

Rodnae Productions. (2021). *A group of women striking a pose [Online Image]*. In Pexels. https://www.pexels.com/photo/a-group-of-women-striking-a-pose-7491157/

SHVETS Production. (2021). *Anonymous female therapist and client sitting in armchairs during session in modern office [Online Image]*. In Pexels. https://www.pexels.com/photo/anonymous-female-therapist-and-client-sitting-in-armchairs-during-session-in-modern-office-7176317/

Vaitkevich, N. (2021). *Matchsticks on the yellow surface [Online Image]*. In Pexels. https://www.pexels.com/photo/matchsticks-on-the-yellow-surface-6837562/

www.ingramcontent.com/pod-product-compliance
Lightning Source LLC
Chambersburg PA
CBHW051703160426
43209CB00004B/998